Conventions used:

<u>Keyboard:</u>
Keys to be pressed are enclosed in parenthesis such as: press (Enter).

Text to be typed, when included in an exercise step will be shaded. For example:
Type *No Fault Travel* and then press (Enter).

<u>Mouse Operations:</u>

Click: refers to clicking the left mouse button

Right-click: refers to clicking the right mouse button

Drag: refers to clicking and holding the left mouse button down and moving the mouse

Be sure to check out our website: www.Pro-aut.com to contact the author and see additional resources available for this workbook.

Published by:

Pro-Aut Training and Consulting, Inc.
1024 Hemlock Ave.
Lewiston, ID 83501

For discounts on quantity orders, check out our website: www.Pro-aut.com

You may also visit www.LutherMaddy.com to contact the author and see additional resources available for this workbook.

Table of Contents

Lesson #1: Getting Started

In this lesson you will learn to:
Move around the Worksheet
Create Basic Formulas
Save Workbooks

Lesson #1: Getting Started

Excel is a spreadsheet program. Spreadsheets are useful primarily for information in which you will perform mathematical computations. Uses for spreadsheets run from simple applications like tracking a family budget, to performing complex financial modeling. One of the advantages of using a spreadsheet is that you can make changes in numeric values and instantly see how that change affects computed values. That allows spreadsheet users to perform "what if" analysis.

Starting Excel

When you start Excel, it allows you to open a workbook you have previously created, create a new blank workbook, or use one of the many pre-defined templates available with Excel 2016. For this course in Excel Basics, you will create workbooks from scratch to allow you to learn more about it. So, the option you want to select when you start Excel is Blank Workbook.

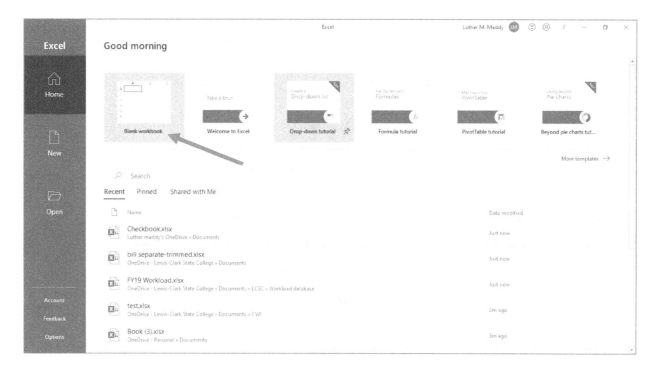

1. **Start Excel if needed and select a Blank Workbook at the startup screen.**

The Excel Window

After selecting the Blank Workbook, you should see a new, blank workbook. Here are some of the items you should be aware of when using Excel.

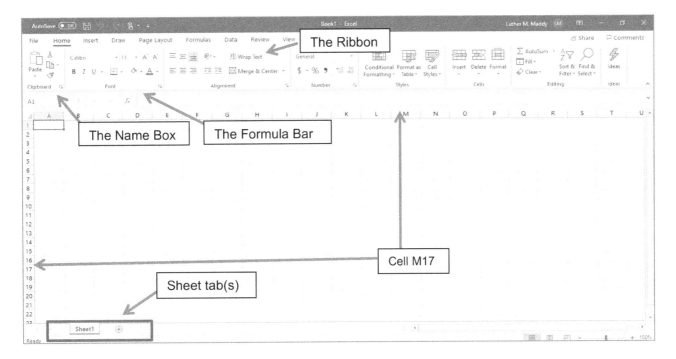

The Ribbon: The Ribbon displays feature tabs. The ribbon allows you access to features related to the tab name. The most commonly used features are found on the Home ribbon.

The Name Box: The name box displays the address or reference of the active cell.

Sheet Tab(s): An Excel workbook may have many worksheets within it. You can think of a sheet as simply another page in the workbook. By default, Excel 2016 starts with one sheet. You will learn to add additional worksheets in a later course.

The Cell: You should notice a series of rows and columns. Each of these rows and columns intersect to form cells. Each cell has a unique address or reference. The cell's address is the column first and then the row. For example, the cell in the top left corner of the worksheet is referred to as A1, column A, row 1. This is verified in the Name Box, or the active cell's address as we referred to it earlier. The active cell also contains the cell pointer.

The Formula Bar:
The formula bar will display the actual contents of a cell. Cells can contain labels, values, dates and formulas. The formula bar will display what is in the cell, the formula for example. The cell itself will display the result of that formula.

Moving Around the Worksheet

The Excel Worksheet consists of 16,384 columns and 1,048,576 rows. This is a very large area of workspace. While you can use the arrow keys to move cell by cell, this is not very efficient if you are working with a large number of cells. To solve this problem, Excel allows you to move to other cells several ways. Among these are:

Page Down	Moves one screen * **down**
Page UP	Moves one screen * **up**
Alt+Page UP	Moves one screen * **left**
Alt+Page Down	Moves one screen * **right**

*How far the active cell indicator actually moves depends on the number of rows or columns you can see on one screen. This is determined by column width, row height and even computer display resolution.

The Go To command

Should you need to move to a cell several screens away, you can use the Go To command. This command will quickly move you to a cell after you type that cell's address.

You can access the Go To command from the Home Tab → Editing → Find & Select. You can also use (F5) to get to the Go To command. One of the quickest ways to access the Go To command is to click in the **Name Box** and then type the address of the cell you want to go to and then press (Enter).

Entering Data in Cells

In this portion of the lesson you will enter data types into cells.

2. In the new workbook, ensure cell A1 is the active cell.

You should see "A1" displayed in the name box and the headings for Column A and row 1 should appear differently than the other row and column headings.

3. In this cell type: *No Fault Travel Profit and Loss Statement* and press (Enter).

When you pressed (Enter), you should have moved down to cell A2.

Working with Long Labels

The text in cell A1 is called a long label. It is called a label because it is text instead of numeric values. It is called a long label because it exceeds the width of the cell in which you typed it.

Long labels can move into cells next to them as long as those cells are empty. If those cells contain data, then the long label cannot move into that cell. Even though the title you just typed appears to be in several cells, it is actually contained completely in cell A1.

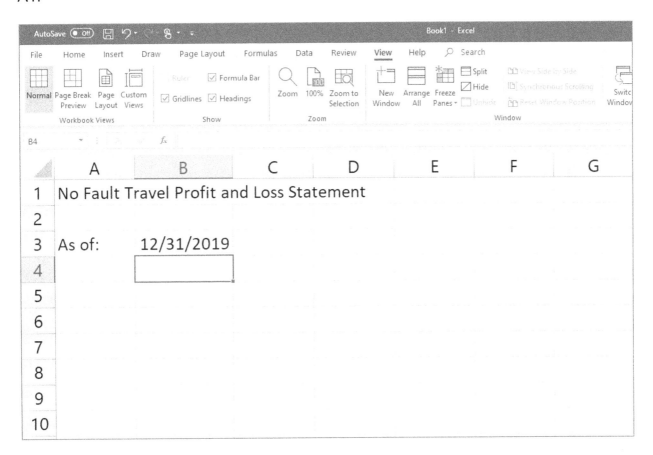

4. **Move to cell A3, type** *As of:* **and then press the (Right) arrow.**

You should now be in cell B3. Pressing a direction key completes the data entry process and moves the active cell indicator in the direction you selected.

5. **In cell B3 type** *12/31/19* **and press (Enter).**

You can enter dates in Excel as you would type them. You can also use dates in computations if needed. If this cell displays ##### instead of the date, Column B is not wide enough. You can ignore this for now, you'll learn to change column width in just a few pages.

6. Move to cell A5 and enter the remaining data to have your worksheet appear as the one below:

Don't add any formatting such as dollar ($) signs. You will add formatting in a later lesson. Be sure to enter the data in the cells as shown.

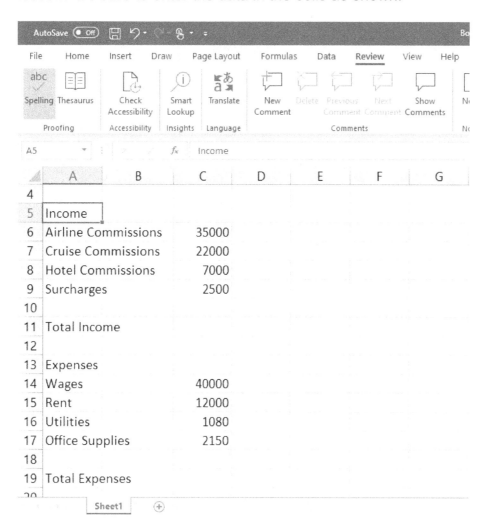

Saving Workbooks

To keep from losing your work you should save at regular intervals. The first time you save you will have to give the file a name. Excel does have an Auto Save feature that will ensure your workbook is saved automatically. Manually saving it the first time allows you to know where the file is stored and what you have named it.

1. Click File on the ribbon to open the File menu, and then choose Save.

Because you have not yet named this file, Excel displays the options for "Save As" rather than "Save". Here you will tell Excel now where you would like to save this file and give it a name. Where you save your documents may differ, but this course will be assuming you are saving in the Documents folder in Microsoft's OneDrive. If you want to choose a different location, you may do so easily by clicking the Browse icon and then choosing a location.

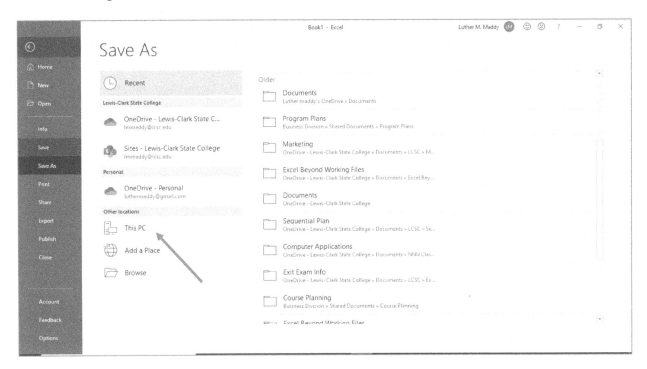

2.   **Choose This PC and then Documents as the location to save this workbook.**

You will now see the Save As dialog box. You will only see this dialog box when you choose the Save command for the first time in a file.

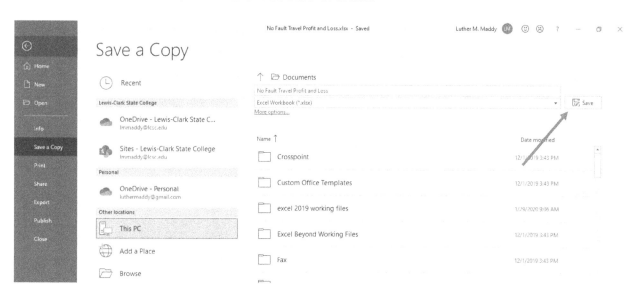

Depending on your version of Windows, your Save As dialog box may appear different than the one above. If you are using a folder other than Documents, make sure you remember where you saved the file so you can find it again.

3.   In the File name text box type, *No Fault Travel Profit and Loss* and then click Save.

You will now return to the worksheet. You should notice the name of the file on the title bar at the top of the Excel window. You can now make additional changes to the spreadsheet and then save it periodically to ensure you do not lose any important work. If the Auto Save feature is on, Excel will save this file automatically for you.

Entering Basic Formulas

Excel is all about formulas and formulas are all about math. Even if you can't add 2+2, that's OK because Excel does the math for you. However, when you are creating your own formulas, you will need to use some basic math, such as knowing which math operations you want to perform and what numbers you want to use in the formula.

If you are somewhat math challenged, you will probably finding creating your own formulas easier than trying to understand some of the formulas you create in this workbook. Follow along with the formulas in the exercises and after you've made it through, you'll probably find creating formulas is nothing to fear.

To enter a formula manually, you will begin it with = and then type the formula. The formula should refer to the cell addresses that you want to compute, not the values in those cells. For example, =B3+B4, not =232+343.

You can use the four basic math functions in Excel formulas, Addition (+), Subtraction (-), Multiplication (*), and Division (/). These symbols are easily accessible on the numeric keypad of the keyboard. The other operation you can perform in Excel formulas is exponentiation. That is raising a value by a certain power, such as 3^2. The exponent symbol is ^ (above the 6 on the keyboard) and is performed before any other calculation in the order of operations.

Order of Operation

When Excel encounters formulas with different operators such as multiplication and addition, there is a certain order in which it performs the computation. To help you remember this order you may try the acronym, "Please Excuse My Dear Aunt Sally". The order of operation is: Parentheses, Exponent, Multiply, or Divide, before Adding or Subtracting. Multiplication and Division have an equal weight, so if there are both, go from left to right. The same is true for Addition and Subtraction. You can change the order of operation by adding parenthesis, (). When Excel sees parenthesis, it performs that part of the formula first.

1.   Move to cell C11.

You can move here by using the arrow keys or by simply clicking in the cell. In this cell you will enter a formula to add all the income sources together.

2.   In this cell type: *=C6+C7+C8+C9* and press (Enter)

The = at the beginning of this formula tells Excel that you are creating a formula. You should now see the total of these values in cell C11.

Using Cell Addresses in Formulas

When you create formulas you could just type the values rather than the cell addresses, =123+456 for example. However, entering a formula this way creates the formula using constant values. If you ever changed the values in the cells from 123 or 456 to

---

something else, the formula would not reflect that change because it is always adding 123 to 456. By using the cell addresses, C6, C7 and so on, if the values in those cells change, the cell with the formula will adjust to the new values. If you had "hard coded" numbers into the formula, you would have to change the formula as well as the numbers to have it display the correct values. Whenever possible, use cell addresses in formulas rather than actual values.

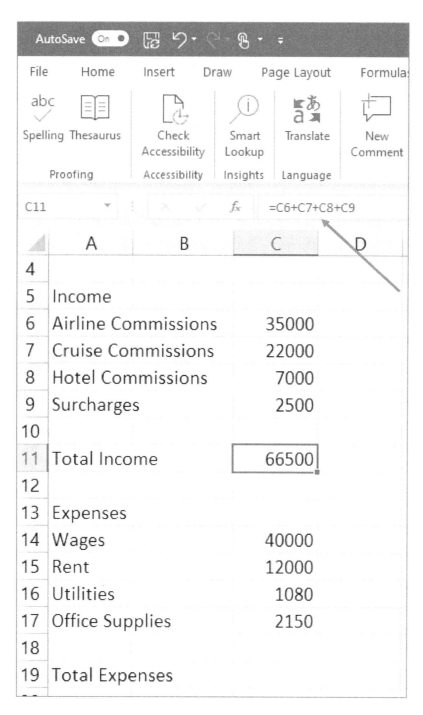

Notice the formula you typed is visible in the formula bar. The result is visible in the cell. The formula bar shows you what is actually in a cell, in this case, a formula. The result of the formula is displayed in the cell itself.

The AutoSum Tool

Entering a formula as you just did could be very tedious, especially in cases where you need to add several values in the same row or column. If you have several values in a row or a column that you want to <u>add</u> together, you can then use Excel's AutoSum tool to create the formula for you. You will now use the AutoSum tool to total the expenses.

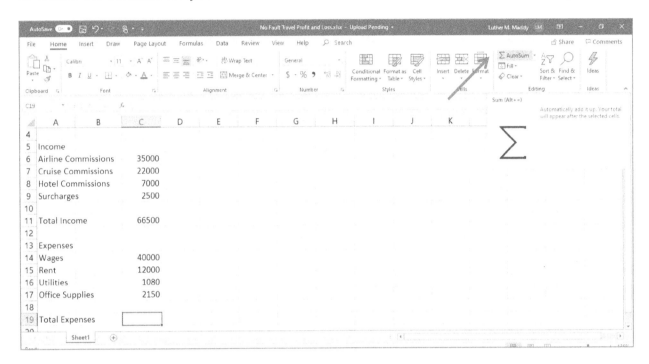

3.   Move to cell C19 and click the AutoSum tool on the Home ribbon.

Excel will now place a marquee around the cells it thinks you want to total. In this case, Excel has guessed correctly. In instances where the cells are not correct, you can click and drag to choose the cells you want to add. After selecting the correct cells, you can simply press (Enter) to complete the formula.

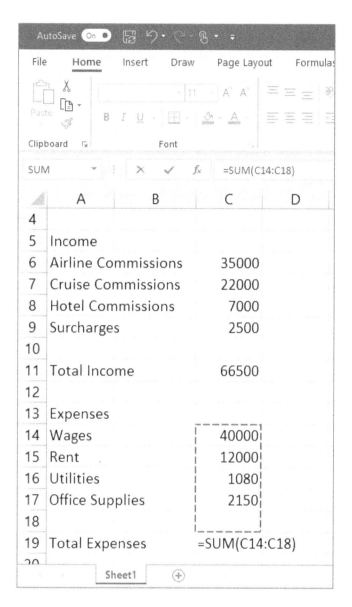

4. Press (Enter) to complete the formula.

You should see a total in cell C19.

The next formula you create will compute the net income for this example company, No Fault Travel. You will do this by having Excel subtract the total expenses from the total income.

5. Move to cell A21 and type *Net Income* and then press the (Right) arrow twice to move to cell C21.

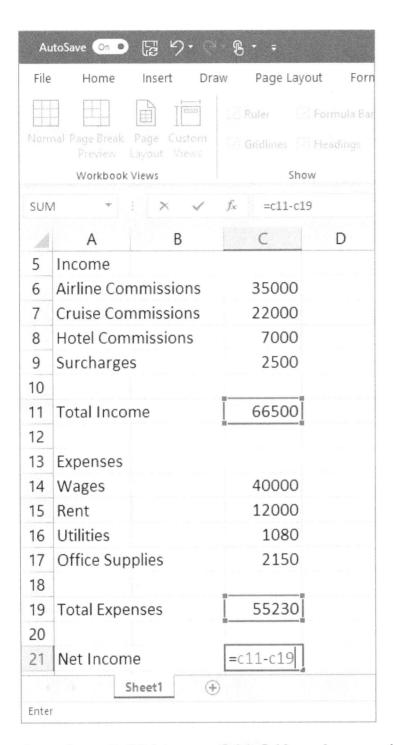

6.   In cell C21 type *=C11-C19* and press (Enter).

The formula you just created subtracts the expenses from the income to compute the company's profit.

7.   Click the File tab and choose Save.

This saves the changes you have just made to the workbook. Notice that you did not have to specify the name again. You only need to give the file a name the first time you save. If you had selected the Save As command, Excel would give you the chance to save the file under a different name. Choosing the Save As command will allow you to confirm that you want to overwrite this file. Using the Save command is the fastest way to continually save a file as you are working on it.

Again, if the Auto Save feature is on, you do not need to do this, but saving periodically is a good habit to acquire for extra protection when you are using programs that do not have the Auto Save feature, or for times when you may have mistakenly turned it off.

You can also use the Quick Access toolbar to save, but just clicking on the icon that resembles a computer disk. You can also see the status of the Auto Save feature here too.

8.   Click the File tab and choose Close.

You have now "put away" this workbook and can now create a new one or open an existing workbook. You will do both in the next lesson.

Skill Builder: Lesson #1

Since you closed the worksheet you just created, you'll need to tell Excel to create a new workbook to create this skill builder lesson.

1. **Click the File tab, click New and then choose Blank workbook.**

2. **Create the spreadsheet on the next page. Create a formula in cell C6 that subtracts the check amount in B6 from the beginning balance in cell C3.**

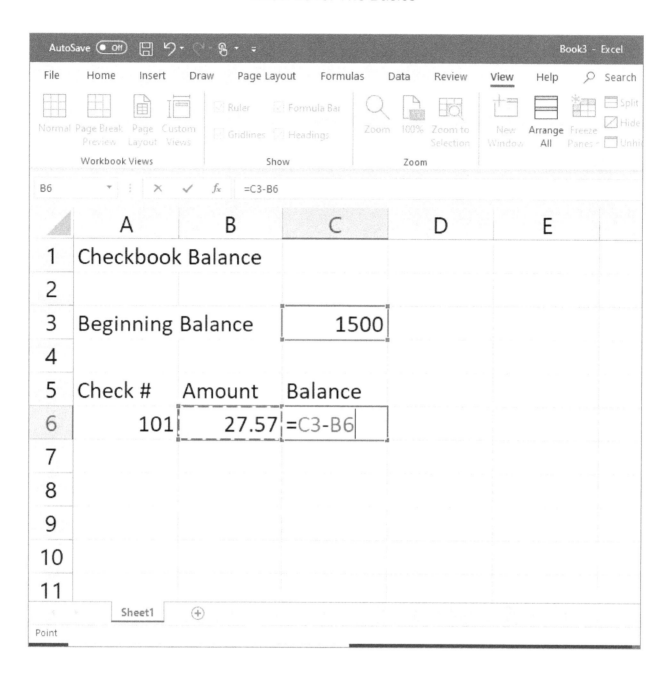

3. Save this workbook as *Checkbook* and then close the file.

Place this file in the same folder as the No Fault Travel workbook.

Lesson #2: Moving & Copying Data and Formulas

In this lesson you will learn to:

Move and Copy Cell Contents
Edit Cell Contents
Use the Fill Handle
Copy Formulas

17

Lesson #2: Moving & Copying Data and Formulas

Excel is a very flexible program. You can easily edit cell contents and move and copy data and values. In this lesson, you will rearrange the spreadsheet by moving and copying. You will also learn about copying formulas and when a formula can be correctly copied and when it cannot.

Opening an Existing Workbook

After closing a workbook, you will need to open it to continue working on it. You'll now open the No Fault Travel Profit and Loss file you created in Lesson #1, to use in this portion of Lesson #2.

1.   Click File and then choose the Open command.

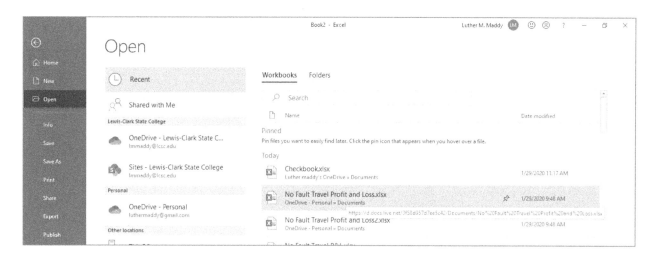

Excel will now list all the Workbook files you have worked on recently. If the file you need is not here you can click the Browse tool and navigate to the correct folder.

2.   Click *No Fault Travel Profit and Loss* in the list of Recent Workbooks to open this file.

You should now see the No Fault Travel P&L workbook just as you left it when you closed it. Excel even remembers which cell was active when you last saved the file. When you open the workbook file, you will notice the active cell may not always be cell A1. The key combination, (Control+Home) will quickly move to cell A1.

Editing Cell Contents

Excel provides several ways of changing or editing cell contents. To replace the entire entry of a cell you can just type over the value you do not want. To change just a portion of a cell's contents you can edit the cell's contents instead of replacing it. To edit a cell's contents move into that cell. Then, click in the Formula bar (Active cell contents) and make the necessary changes.

1.   **Move to cell C8, the value for Hotel Commissions type *9847,* then press (Enter).**

You replaced the old contents with the new value. Notice also that the total income and net income also changed automatically to reflect the new value. This is because you created the formulas using cell addresses.

2.   **Move to cell C16, the value for Utilities.**

This time you will leave most of the existing contents intact and simply edit this value instead of replacing it.

3.   **Click at the end of this cell's contents in the Formula bar.**

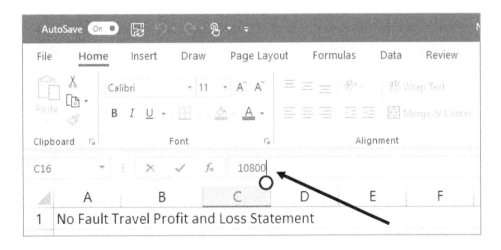

4.   **After you see the insertion point (cursor) blinking at the end of the current value, type a *0* to change the value to 10800 and then press (Enter).**

As it did before, Excel will update all the formulas to reflect this change.

Selecting Cells

Before you can move or copy cells, you must first select those cells. By selecting cells, you inform Excel which cells you wish to move or copy. You will also need to select cells for many other operations, such as format changes.

There are several ways to select cells. The most basic is to click and drag. However, to select cells, start in the middle of that cell. When you are in the correct place for selecting cells, the mouse pointer will resemble a white plus symbol (✢).

Should you wish to select an entire column or row, you can click on the column or row heading to select every cell in that row or column. Should you wish to select more than one entire column, you can do so by clicking and dragging to select multiple column or row headings.

In addition to using the mouse, you can also select cells with the keyboard. To do this, move to the first cell you wish to select. Then, press and hold the (Shift) key and then press an arrow key in the direction you want to select. As long as the (Shift) key is depressed, any movement command will highlight cells.

Selecting non-contiguous ranges

Sometimes you may need to select groups of cells that are not together. To select non-contiguous groups of cells, select the first group of cells with the mouse. Then, press and hold the (Control) key and then select the second group of cells. As long as you hold down the (Control) key, you can select as many separate ranges as you wish.

1.　　Move to cell A3.

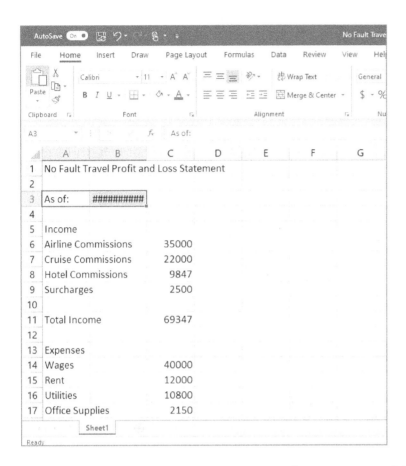

2.　　Ensure that the mouse pointer resembles a white plus (⊕) and then click and drag to cell B3.

You should notice that the cell you started with is not shaded. However, the thick black border tells you that both cells are selected. Excel leaves the starting cell white so you know where you started selecting cells.

3.　　Press (Delete) to delete the contents of the selected cells.

You have now deleted the date and the date label. The (Delete) key will delete the contents of all selected cells. If only one cell is active, it will delete that one cell's contents. Remember the ####'s in the cell indicate the column must be wider to display that cell's contents.

4.　　Move to cell C11 and press (Delete).

As you saw earlier, the AutoSum formula was a better approach to adding a column of numbers than entering the formula that contained a reference to each cell to be added. You will now replace the formula you created by using the AutoSum feature.

5.   Click the AutoSum tool Σ AutoSum ▾ **on the Home tab and then press (Enter).**

The amount in the calculated cell will be the same as before, however, this formula is much better in the long run as you will see in future lessons. If you move into this cell and view the formula, you will see that it sums adds C6 through C10. The colon (:) represents "through". This means, as you will see later, if you insert additional rows between C6 and C10, the values you enter will be included in the total.

Moving Cells

To move cells from one location to another the first step is to select the cells you want to move. After selecting those cells, you then choose the Cut command. After choosing the Cut command, move where you want the new cells to appear. After moving to the new destination, choose the Paste command.

One thing that can make the moving and copying process somewhat complex is the several methods available for accessing the Cut, Copy and Paste commands. For example you can find these commands the following ways:

    On the Home tab in the clipboard group.
    Right-clicking on selected cells.
    Keyboard shortcut keys:
        (Control+x) = Cut, (Control+c) = Copy, & (Control+v) = Paste

There is no right or wrong way to select a command. Most commands in Excel can be executed multiple ways. The best method of selecting a command is the one you remember. However, after you become more comfortable with Excel, you'll probably want to become more efficient at it. Then, learning more than one way of performing an operation will save time.

1.   Use the click and drag method to select cells A5:C21.

Excel uses (:) to represent "through". Remember that to select cells the mouse pointer must resemble the white plus symbol.

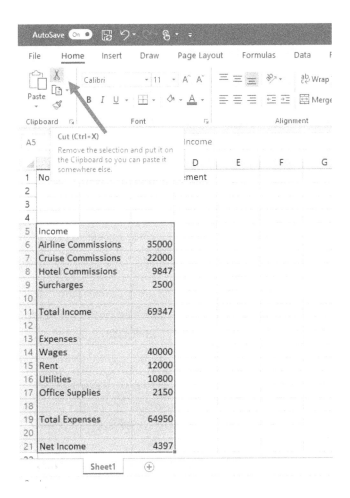

2. **With these cells selected, click the Cut tool on the ribbon on the Home tab.**

Unlike other programs you may use, the selected cells do not disappear when you choose the Cut command. Instead, Excel places a marquee around the cells so you know which ones will move. The process will not be complete until you actually choose the Paste command. You may have also noticed that when you pointed to the Cut tool Excel display more information about that command, including the keyboard shortcut, (Control+X), that you could have also used.

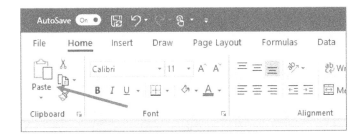

3. **Click in cell A4 and then click the Paste tool on the Home tab.**

The Paste tool has a drop down arrow, but you do not need to use that now. Clicking the tool icon will cause Excel to paste the cells you cut, beginning at cell A4.

All of the selected cells will now move up one row. As discussed earlier, you could have also accessed the Cut and Paste command using any of the additional methods Excel provides with the same results.

The cells you moved contained three cells with formulas. As you moved these cells, Excel automatically adjusted the formulas to fit their new location. For example, the formula that computed the new income was =C11-C19. If you examine this cell now, you will see that Excel adjusted the formula to become =C10-C18. This is one of the most powerful features of Excel. When you move, insert, or delete cells, Excel will automatically adjust the formulas in the worksheet.

Using the Fill Handle

The fill handle (the skinny black plus at the right edge of the active cell) provides a very quick way to copy a cell's contents. It is particularly useful for copying formulas.

Another feature of the fill handle is that it will attempt to increment text values such as months or days of the week. This is very useful if you are creating column headings representing several consecutive months. You'll use the fill handle now to create headings for additional months of the year. You'll also use it to copy formulas.

1.   Move to cell C3 and type *Jan*.

It's not necessary to press (Enter) after typing Jan. If you do, you'll need to move back into cell C3.

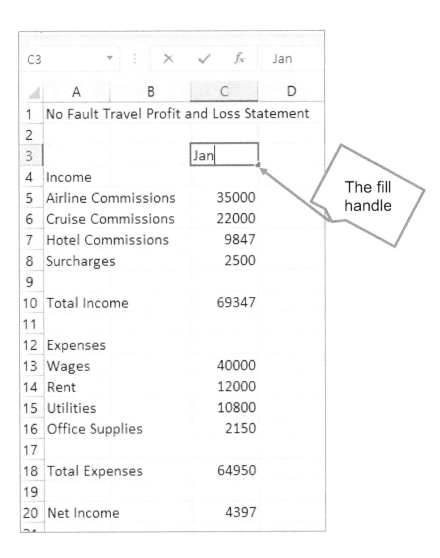

The fill handle

2. Locate the fill handle at the bottom right corner of cell C3.

When you are in the correct location, the mouse pointer will resemble a small black plus symbol.

3. Click and drag the fill handle to cell H3 and then release the mouse.

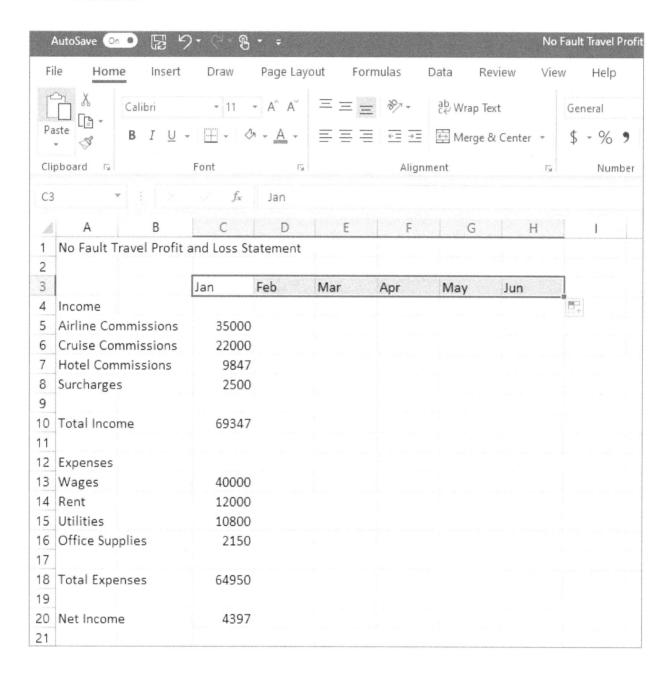

Excel will then fill the cells you selected, incrementing month names. If cell C3 had contained January, Excel would have incremented the other cells with the full month names as well. The fill handle increments month names, days of the week, and numeric patterns.

Copying Formulas

One of the most common things to copy in Excel are formulas. For example, in the spreadsheet you are currently creating, you will need formulas to compute the total income, total expenses, and net income for each month. Creating each of these formulas separately would be very time consuming.

In situations where you need several formulas, you may be able to copy an existing formula. When you copy a formula, you are not copying the formula itself, but instead are copying what the formula does, relative to the cell where the formula is located.

Unless you tell Excel otherwise it will adjust as you copy the formula. For instance, the formula in cell C20 (the net income) is =C10-C18. Copying that formula to cell D20 will cause Excel to change the references from C to D. Once copied to cell D20, the formula would change to =D10-D18. The formula does the same thing when you copy it. It subtracts the total expenses from the total income, in the column you copied it to. Excel adjusts formula when you copy them to fit their new location.

This feature allows you to copy formulas that do the same thing many times. Just remember that the only formulas that can be copied without making adjustments are formulas that will do the exact same thing in relation to the cell with the formula, but in a different location. As in the example discussed in the previous paragraph, the formula is always subtracting a cell two rows above the cell with the formula from the cell twelve rows above that cell, no matter where you copy that formula to.

In the example worksheet, the formulas for total income, total expenses, and net income are all formulas that can be copied because you do want them to do the same computations in the place they are copied to was the formula did when you created it. You will use the fill handle to make the copy process even easier.

1.   **Move to cell C10.**

2.   **Locate the fill handle in the lower right corner of this cell.**

3.   **Drag the fill handle to cell H10.**

You should now see zeros in the cells where you just copied the formula. As you enter data into the income cells for each month, the formulas will display different values.

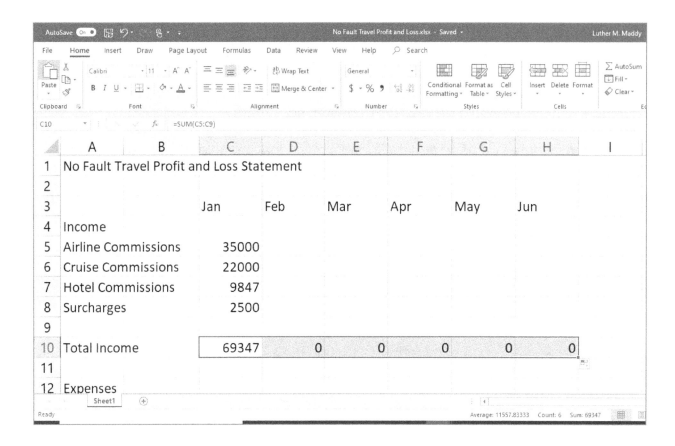

4. Use the fill handle to copy the formulas located in cells C18 and C20 to H18 and H20 as shown.

These cells will also display zero values because there are no values in the cells the new formulas refer to. As soon as you add some values for the additional months, the cells with the formulas will display values too.

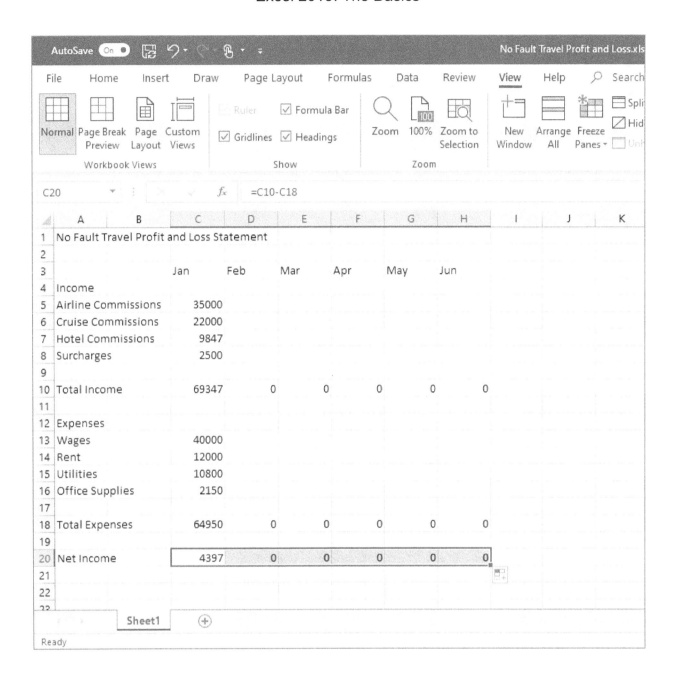

5. Save the file but leave it open.

Saving the workbook periodically prevents losing data in case of a power outage or computer glitch. Even with the Auto Save feature on, it is a good idea to save manually often, especially after changing something significant or before closing the file, just in case.

6.   Enter the additional values as shown below:

H17	▼	⋮	✕	✓	*fx*			

◢	A	B	C	D	E	F	G	H	I
3			Jan	Feb	Mar	Apr	May	Jun	
4	Income								
5	Airline Commissions		35000	40200	35000	42500	40000	40000	
6	Cruise Commissions		22000	18000	12000	17000	20000	21000	
7	Hotel Commissions		9847	11000	8000	9000	8000	9000	
8	Surcharges		2500	1800	1000	1800	1500	2500	
9									
10	Total Income		69347	71000	56000	70300	69500	72500	
11									
12	Expenses								
13	Wages		40000	41000	39000	40000	43000	39000	
14	Rent		12000	12000	12000	12000	12000	12000	
15	Utilities		10800	11000	9000	10000	8000	10000	
16	Office Supplies		2150	1800	1500	2000	1900	2000	
17									
18	Total Expenses		64950	65800	61500	64000	64900	63000	
19									
20	Net Income		4397	5200	-5500	6300	4600	9500	
21									

Sheet1   ⊕

Ready

As you enter these values, do not enter anything in the cells with formulas in them. You should notice that the cells with the formulas in them change as you enter values in that column.

7.   After entering the data, move to cell A1 with (Control+Home) and then Save and close the workbook.

When you save an Excel workbook, Excel remembers the active cell's location. Then, when you open the workbook again, Excel takes you to the cell that was active when you saved the workbook. In other words, Excel takes you right back where you were working. You moved to cell A1 before saving so you would be in this cell when you open the saved workbook again.

Skill builder: Lesson #2

1.   Open the *Checkbook* workbook.

2.   Move cells C5:C6 to D5:D6.

You are moving the balance over one column to the right. You may try the drag and drop method for moving. To do this, select the cells then move the mouse pointer to any edge of the selected cells (the mouse pointer will include a four headed arrow). Then, click and drag the cells to the new location.

3.   In cell C5 enter a label of *Description*.

Column C is not wide enough to display the entire label you just entered. You will correct this in a later lesson.

4.   Use the fill handle to copy the formula in cell D6 to D7 through D20.

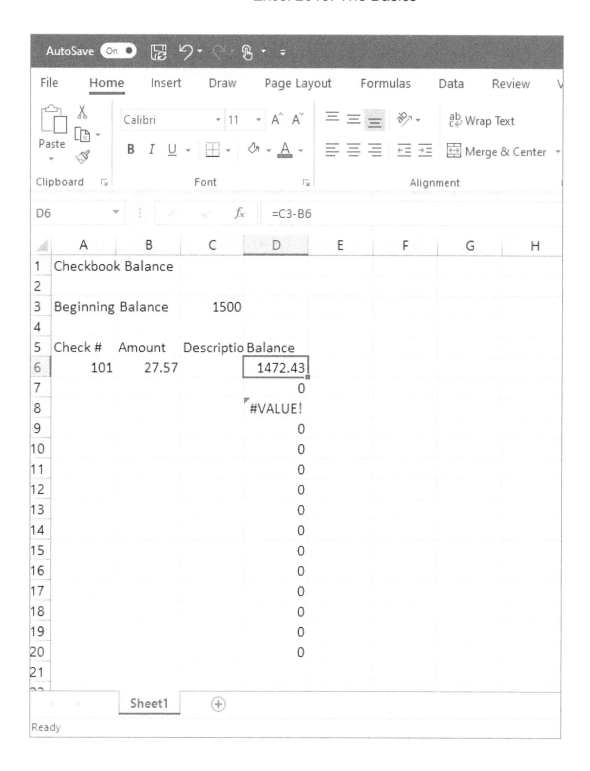

You will get an error message in one of these cells. This is because this formula, as it is now, is not a formula that can be correctly copied. This problem will be corrected in the next lesson.

5. Save and close the file.

Lesson #3: Using Functions and Absolute Reference

In this lesson you will learn to:
> *Use Basic Functions*
> *Use Absolute Reference in Formulas*

Lesson #3: Using Functions and Absolute Reference

Excel provides several shortcuts when you are creating what could be fairly complex formulas. So far, you have already used one Excel function, the Sum function. As you should recall, the Sum function made it possible to add several cells in a very simple formula.

In addition to the Sum function, Excel has numerous other functions. In this lesson you will explore some of Excel's basic functions. After you've done that, you'll then learn more about copying formulas and you'll learn the important feature called Absolute Reference.

1.   Open the *No Fault Travel P&L* workbook.

The Go to Command

You can use the mouse to quickly click and go to any cell you see. However, if you wish to quickly move to a cell you cannot see, even one that is quite far away, you can use the Go to command.

The easiest way to access the Go to command is from the name box. To move to another cell, just type that cell's address in the name box and press (Enter). Excel will then instantly move you to that cell. You can also access the Go to command with the F5 function key.

2.   Click in the Name box, type *A23* and then press (Enter).

Be sure that you don't put a space between the A and the 23.

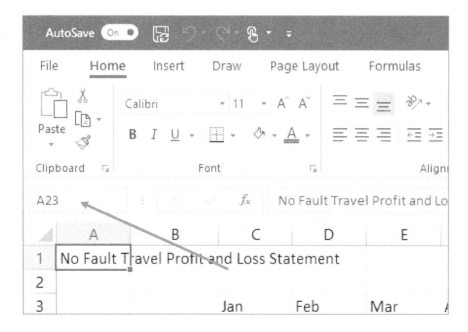

As you pressed (Enter), Excel moved the active cell to A23.

3.   In cell A23 type, *Total Monthly Income* and press the (Right) arrow twice to move to cell C23.

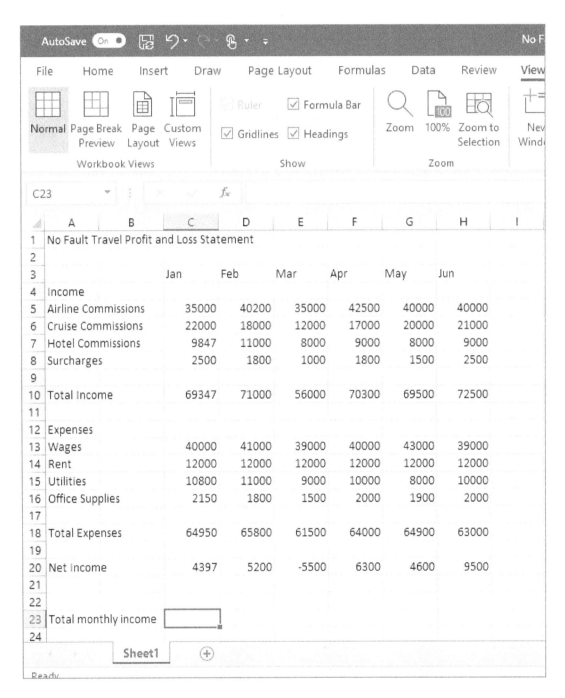

When you used the Sum function earlier, you used the AutoSum tool. This tool simply adds all the values it sees above or to the left of the current cell. In this case, you will use the Sum function but manually inform Excel which cells to add.

4. In cell C23 type =*Sum(C20:H20)* and press (Enter).

The parentheses () are a necessary component when using functions of any kind.

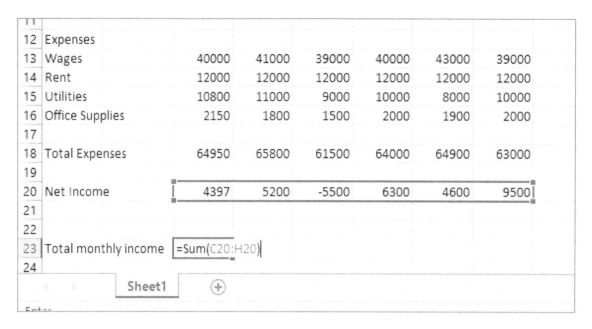

12	Expenses						
13	Wages	40000	41000	39000	40000	43000	39000
14	Rent	12000	12000	12000	12000	12000	12000
15	Utilities	10800	11000	9000	10000	8000	10000
16	Office Supplies	2150	1800	1500	2000	1900	2000
17							
18	Total Expenses	64950	65800	61500	64000	64900	63000
19							
20	Net Income	4397	5200	-5500	6300	4600	9500
21							
22							
23	Total monthly income	=Sum(C20:H20)					
24							

Sheet1 ⊕

Enter

This formula will add all the monthly incomes together.

Using additional functions

There are many additional functions available for you to use in Excel. In this portion of the lesson you will use the Average, Max, and Min functions. These functions are readily available from the drop down list button on the AutoSum tool.

1. Move to cell A24 and type *Average Monthly Profit* and press (Right) twice to move to cell C24.

You may not be able to see all of the text you just typed. Don't worry about this, you will learn to increase column widths in the next lesson.

2. Locate and click the arrow just to the right of the AutoSum tool on the toolbar. Then, click <u>Average</u> from the drop down list.

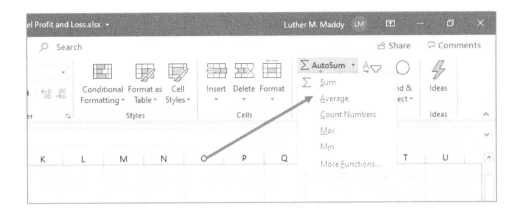

Excel will now place the Average function in cell C24. Excel tries to guess which cells you want to average, which in this case is not correct. The next step is to tell Excel which cells you want to average which, for this worksheet, are cells C20 : H20. You can now either type those cells into the formula within the parenthesis or click and drag to select the cells. For example purposes, you'll select the cells to be averaged by clicking and dragging.

3. Select cells C20 through H20 by clicking and dragging.

Be sure to select cells using the "fat white plus" in the middle of the cell.

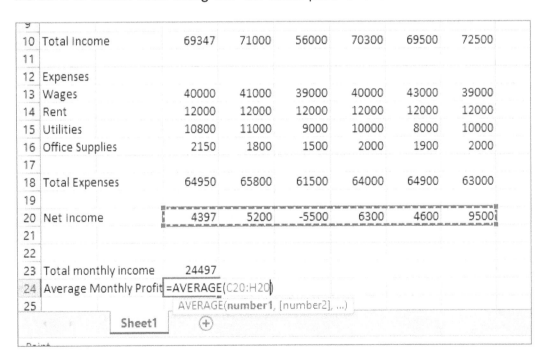

9						
10	Total Income	69347	71000	56000	70300	69500	72500
11						
12	Expenses					
13	Wages	40000	41000	39000	40000	43000	39000
14	Rent	12000	12000	12000	12000	12000	12000
15	Utilities	10800	11000	9000	10000	8000	10000
16	Office Supplies	2150	1800	1500	2000	1900	2000
17						
18	Total Expenses	64950	65800	61500	64000	64900	63000
19						
20	Net Income	4397	5200	-5500	6300	4600	9500
21						
22						
23	Total monthly income	24497				
24	Average Monthly Profit	=AVERAGE(C20:H20)				
25		AVERAGE(**number1**, [number2], ...)				

Sheet1 ⊕

When you release the mouse you will see a marquee around those cells. You will also see C20:H20 has been added to the Average function in cell C24.

4.   Press (Enter) to complete the formula.

You should now see the average net income in cell C24. The formula bar will display the formula based on the Average function.

5.   Move to cell A25 and type *Highest Monthly Profit* and then move to cell C25.

You will now use the Max function to display the largest monthly profit value.

6.   Click the arrow just to the right of the AutoSum tool on the toolbar and choose <u>Max</u> from the drop down list.

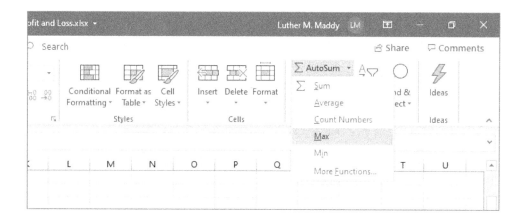

7.   Select cells C20 through H20 by clicking and dragging and then press (Enter).

8.   In cell A26 type, *Lowest Monthly Profit.* Then, using the drop down list by the AutoSum tool, insert the Min function. Select cells C20 through H20 and press (Enter).

You should now have formulas that compute the total, average, maximum, and minimum monthly profit values.

16 Office Supplies	2150	1800	1500	2000	1900	2000
17						
18 Total Expenses	64950	65800	61500	64000	64900	63000
19						
20 Net Income	4397	5200	-5500	6300	4600	9500
21						
22						
23 Total monthly income	24497					
24 Average Monthly Profit	4082.83					
25 Highest Monthly Profit	9500					
26 Lowest Monthly Profit	-5500					
27						
28						

Sheet1 (+)

Ready

Even though the contents of these cells appear to extend into column B, the entire contents are actually in column A. These are examples of "long labels".

9. Move to cell A21 and type *% of Total Income* and then press (Right) twice.

You will now create a formula that computes the percentage January contributed to the total profit for the six-month period. Eventually you will compute the percentages for each of the six months.

10. In cell C21 enter the following formula: *=C20/C23*.

This formula divides January's profit by the total profit for all six months.

	A	B	C	D	E	F	G	H
13	Wages		40000	41000	39000	40000	43000	39000
14	Rent		12000	12000	12000	12000	12000	12000
15	Utilities		10800	11000	9000	10000	8000	10000
16	Office Supplies		2150	1800	1500	2000	1900	2000
17								
18	Total Expenses		64950	65800	61500	64000	64900	63000
19								
20	Net Income		4397	5200	-5500	6300	4600	9500
21	% of total income		=C20/C23					
22								
23	Total monthly income		24497					
24	Average Monthly Profit		4082.83					
25	Highest Monthly Profit		9500					
26	Lowest Monthly Profit		-5500					
27								
28								

Sheet1 (+)

12. Press (Enter) to complete this formula.

Excel should display a value close to 0.179. This value is actually 17.9%. You'll add the percentage formatting in a future lesson.

13. Use the Fill handle and copy this formula into cells D21 through H21.

Remember the Fill handle is the "skinny black plus".

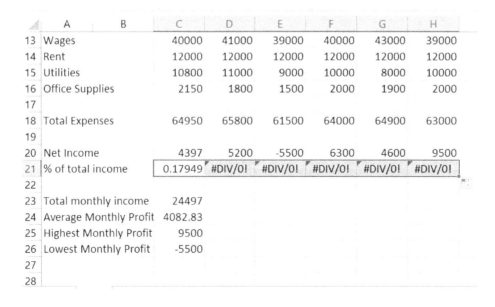

	A	B	C	D	E	F	G	H
13	Wages		40000	41000	39000	40000	43000	39000
14	Rent		12000	12000	12000	12000	12000	12000
15	Utilities		10800	11000	9000	10000	8000	10000
16	Office Supplies		2150	1800	1500	2000	1900	2000
17								
18	Total Expenses		64950	65800	61500	64000	64900	63000
19								
20	Net Income		4397	5200	-5500	6300	4600	9500
21	% of total income		0.17949	#DIV/0!	#DIV/0!	#DIV/0!	#DIV/0!	#DIV/0!
22								
23	Total monthly income		24497					
24	Average Monthly Profit		4082.83					
25	Highest Monthly Profit		9500					
26	Lowest Monthly Profit		-5500					
27								
28								

Using Absolute Reference

The result of copying the formula into cells D21 through H21 is an error message. You have received this error message because this formula is not a formula that can be correctly copied. You may recall that when you copy a formula, you copy what the formula does in relation to the cell where you copy it to.

In other words, the formula in C21 is C20/C23. Excel actually sees this as: divide the cell immediately above this cell (C20) by the cell two below this cell (C23). If you examine the formula in cell D21 you will see that it became D20/D23 when you copied it. Excel replicated the exact relationship the formula represented and adjusted the cells to the new cell. This is what formulas are supposed to do when you copy them, but this is not the result you are after.

Examining the formulas in E21 through H21 will reveal that each formula refers to two cells in the same column in which the formula is located. The actual error message is telling you that you are trying to divide by zero, a mathematical "no no". There is no data in cells D23 through H23.

In this situation, you don't want every part of the formula to change. Instead you'll need every formula to always refer to the one cell that contains the Total Monthly Profit, cell C23. There are two solutions to this problem. One is to manually change each formula to refer to cell C23. The second, and preferred solution, is to change the way Excel treats C23 when it copies the formula.

Since you want all the other formulas to refer to C23 when you copy the formula to the other cells, you need to tell Excel to keep it constant, or absolute, when the formula is copied. You will not change the way Excel treats C21 because you do want this to change to D21 and so on.

The feature to do this is called absolute reference. In a formula, absolute reference is indicated with ($). For example C21/$C$23 would keep C23 as a constant when you copy that formula.

You can change a cell to an absolutely referenced cell either by typing the dollar signs in manually or by using (F4). In this portion of the lesson you will use absolute reference to make the formula in cell C21 one that can be copied.

1.   **Move back into cell C21 and click at the far right end of its formula on the formula bar.**

2.   **With the insertion point blinking at the end of the formula, press (F4).**

The F4 key adds dollar signs ($) before the row and the column. This key is a shortcut key for making a cell absolute. You can also simply add the dollar signs yourself by editing the formula. The dollar sign before the row and column tell Excel not to change this portion of the formula at all when you copy it.

There are variations of the absolute reference. For example, $C23 would tell Excel to keep column C constant but change the row when you copy to a new location. Likewise, C$23 would keep the row constant. For this formula, you want all the other places you copy it to refer to the total of all the monthly incomes in cell C23. To do this requires a dollar sign ($) before the column and the row.

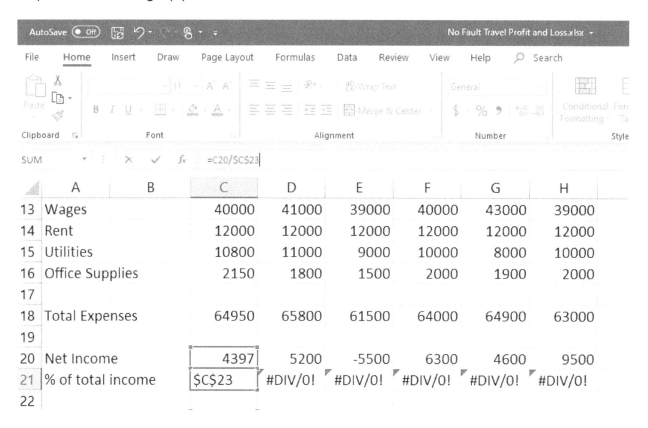

Making cell C23 absolute in the formulas in cells D21 through H21 will cause Excel to display the correct percentage. You can now correctly copy the revised formula.

3.   Use the fill handle to copy the corrected formula from C21 to D21 through H21.

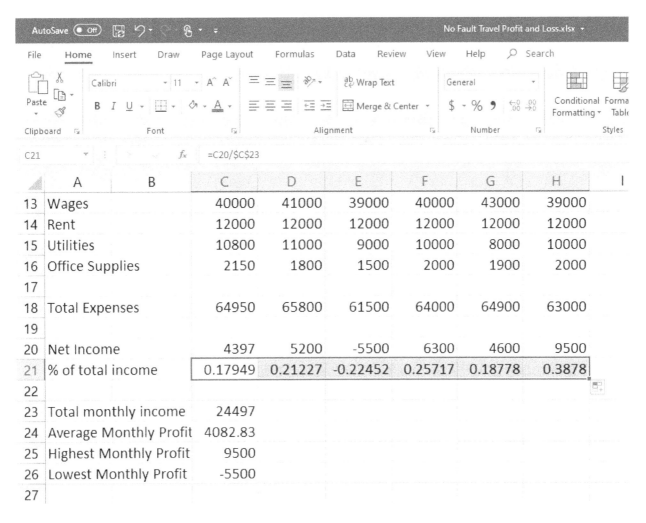

This time you are able to copy the formula with correct results because you used absolute reference. You will add percentage formatting, (%), in an upcoming lesson.

4. Examine the formulas in cell D21 through H21.

Notice that each of these formulas now refers to cell C23. C23 did not change this time when you copied the formula because it was absolutely referenced.

5. Save and close the *No Fault Travel P&L* workbook.

Skill Builder: Lesson #3

1.   Open the *Checkbook* workbook.

2.   Examine the formula in cell D7. Make the necessary corrections to make this worksheet correctly compute a checkbook balance when a check amount is entered in cell B7.

The formula should subtract the check amount from the balance after writing the last check (D6-B7).

3.   After correcting the formula in cell D7, copy the corrected formula from D7 to D8 through D20.

You can correctly copy this formula now because the formulas in the additional rows, 7 through 20, are doing the same thing relative to the cell with the formula. In other words, the formulas in these cells are subtracting the check amount in the same row from the previous balance, directly above the cell with the formula. The first balance uses a balance that is not directly above the cell.

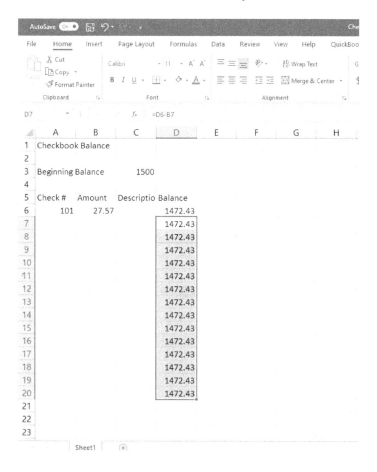

Correcting the formulas in this worksheet did not require using the absolute reference feature. Instead it required creating a formula that did the same thing, relative to the cell with the formula, to compute the new balance.

4.   In cell D1 type: *Total of Checks Written*.

5.   In cell G

1 use the Sum() function to create a formula that will display the total of all the checks written.

Hint: You only need to account for checks up to row 20. That formula will be =Sum(B6:B20)

6.   Enter the additional data as shown below to test your formulas.

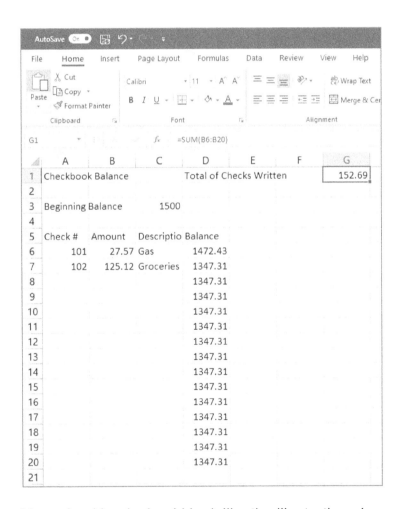

Your checkbook should look like the illustration above.

7.   Save and close the *Checkbook* workbook.

Lesson #4: Formatting Worksheets

In this lesson you will learn to:

Insert Rows and Columns
Change Column Width
Use Numeric Formatting
Change Cell Alignment

Lesson #4: Formatting Worksheets

Inserting and Deleting Rows and Columns

If, after nearly completing your worksheet you realize you need additional rows or columns you can easily add them. However, realize that adding a row does so for the entire worksheet. As you add columns or rows Excel will automatically adjust the formulas that need to change. You can also delete columns you may no longer need. In deleting rows or columns you are just shifting your worksheet data up or to the left. The column letter or row number does not disappear, just the information in that row or column. In this lesson you will insert an additional income category in the No Fault Travel spreadsheet.

1.   Open the *No Fault Travel Profit and Loss* workbook.

2.   Move to the row heading for row 7 and right-click.

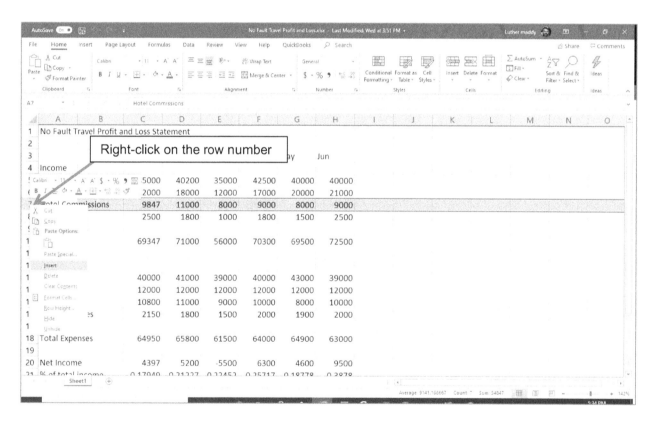

You should now see a shortcut menu. This menu allows you to insert additional rows or to delete this row.

3.   From the shortcut menu click Insert.

Excel should have added a new blank row and moved all data below row 7. All formulas affected by the addition of this row have been updated automatically by Excel.

4. In the new row 7, type *Car Rental Commissions* in A7.

Once again you have entered a long label. You will correct this shortly.

5. Enter *5000* for each month for this new income category.

You should notice that the 5000 amount for car rental commissions is also included in the total income. This would not have happened if you had not changed this formula to use the Sum() function. The formula in C11, the total for the month, adjusted automatically to include the car rental commissions.

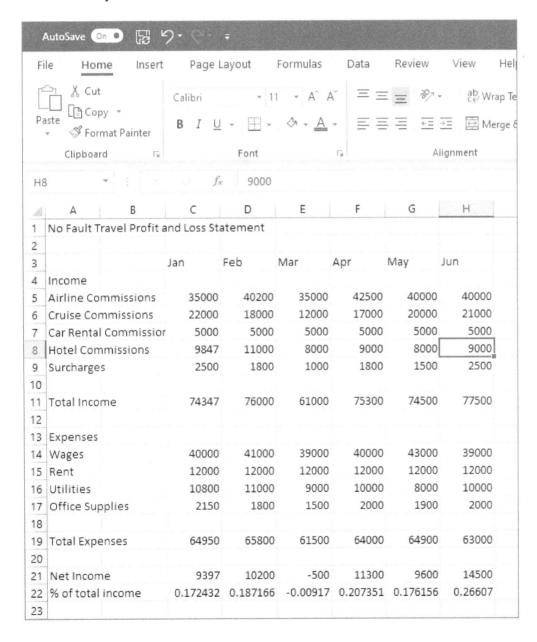

	A	B	C	D	E	F	G	H
1	No Fault Travel Profit and Loss Statement							
2								
3			Jan	Feb	Mar	Apr	May	Jun
4	Income							
5	Airline Commissions		35000	40200	35000	42500	40000	40000
6	Cruise Commissions		22000	18000	12000	17000	20000	21000
7	Car Rental Commissior		5000	5000	5000	5000	5000	5000
8	Hotel Commissions		9847	11000	8000	9000	8000	9000
9	Surcharges		2500	1800	1000	1800	1500	2500
10								
11	Total Income		74347	76000	61000	75300	74500	77500
12								
13	Expenses							
14	Wages		40000	41000	39000	40000	43000	39000
15	Rent		12000	12000	12000	12000	12000	12000
16	Utilities		10800	11000	9000	10000	8000	10000
17	Office Supplies		2150	1800	1500	2000	1900	2000
18								
19	Total Expenses		64950	65800	61500	64000	64900	63000
20								
21	Net Income		9397	10200	-500	11300	9600	14500
22	% of total income		0.172432	0.187166	-0.00917	0.207351	0.176156	0.26607
23								

Changing Cell Alignment

By default, Excel left aligns all labels. You can easily change the alignment of a cell with the formatting tools on the ribbon. For some alignment options you will need to use the Format dialog box. In this portion of the exercise you will change cell alignment.

1.   **Select cells C3 through H3 by clicking and dragging.**

3.   **With these cells selected, locate and click the Center tool on the Home tab of the ribbon.**

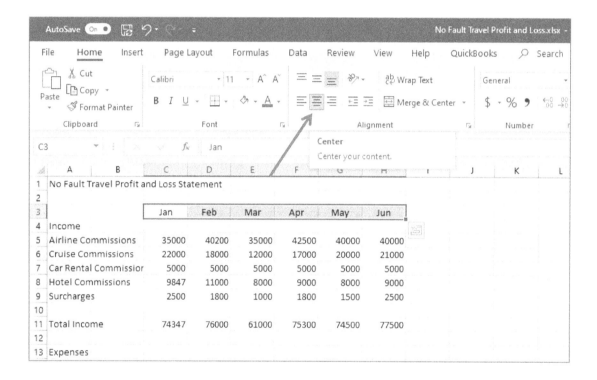

The labels for each month are now centered in their cells.

Changing Column Width

Rather than having long labels move into neighboring cells, you may want to simply increase the width of the column. Excel provides two basic ways to adjust column width, best fit and manual. With the best fit method, Excel will automatically adjust the column to fit the largest label or value it finds in the column. With the manual method, you decide how wide the column should be by dragging.

1.   Move the mouse between the headings for columns A and B.

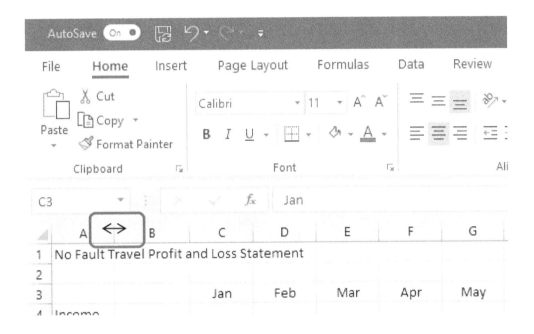

When you are in the correct location, the mouse pointer will appear as a black plus with arrows pointing left and right.

2.   Double-click between the column headings.

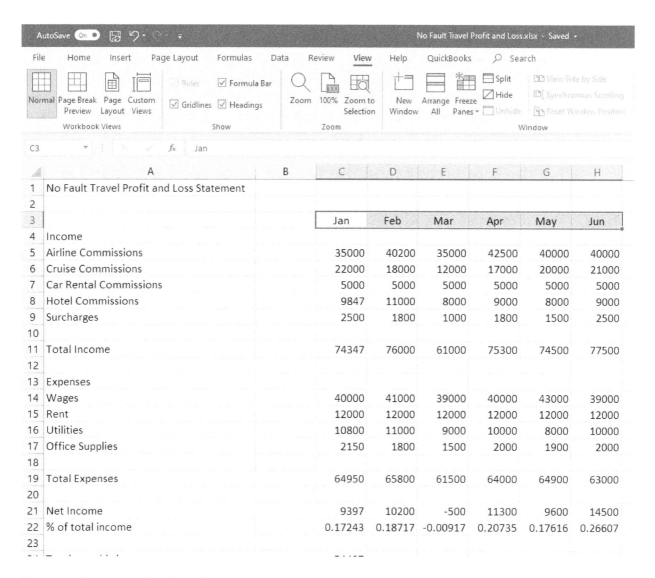

Excel will automatically adjust column A so that the longest label in the column fits. However, adjusting to the longest label in this case makes the column too wide. You will now use the manual method to reduce the size of this column.

3.   Move to the border between the headings for columns A and B. When you see the black plus ←|→, click and drag to the left. Adjust the column to a width of 21.00 characters.

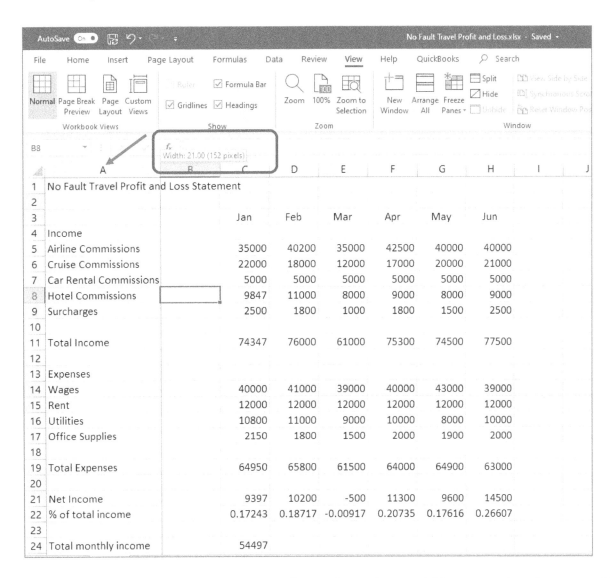

As you drag the column border, you will see the column width appear in a box near the top of the column heading.

Using Merge & Center

The Center command you just used centers cell contents within the cell. This command would have little or undesirable results when used with labels that exceed the boundaries of their cell. If you wish to center a long label within several cells Excel provides the Merge & Center command.

1.   Select cells A1 through H1.

To use the Merge & Center command, first select the cells you want the text to be centered within. Remember to use the "white plus" to select cells.

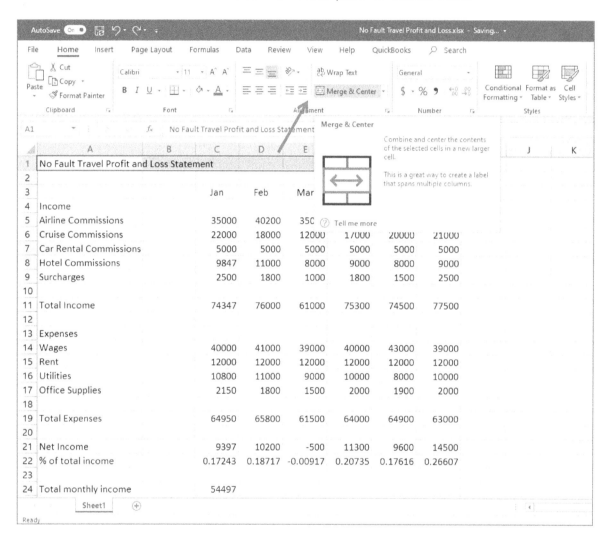

2.   After selecting these cells, locate and click the Merge and Center tool on the Home ribbon.

The cells you selected have now become one large cell. The heading is now centered in the new larger cell.

Column B is now an "extra" column. You'll now delete this column and, as you do this, Excel will automatically adjust all the formulas so they will still work.

3. Right-click column B's heading and choose Delete from the shortcut menu.

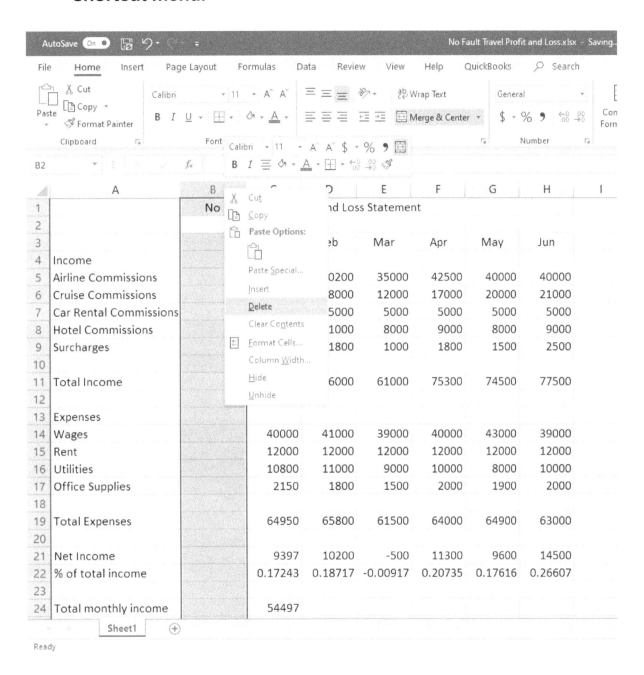

After you clicked Delete, Excel essentially moved all the other data over one column. You should notice all the formulas still compute correctly.

Rotating Text

Excel provides a very easy way to rotate text. This makes it very easy to create impressive spreadsheets.

1.   Select cells B3 through G3.

You will rotate the month names in this worksheet.

2.   Click the Orientation tool in the Alignment group.

3.   Select Angle Counterclockwise.

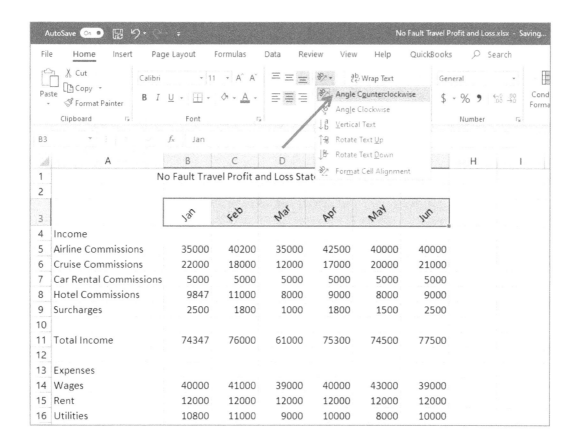

The month names should now be rotated 45 degrees.

Numeric Formatting

Excel has several numeric formatting options that you can easily add to values. You can access accounting (currency), percentage, and comma formatting from the ribbon. Several other numeric and date formatting options are available from the Format Cells dialog box.

1. Select cells B5 through G21 and then click the Accounting style tool ($) in the Number group in the Home tab on the ribbon.

The values in the cells you selected should now appear with currency formatting.

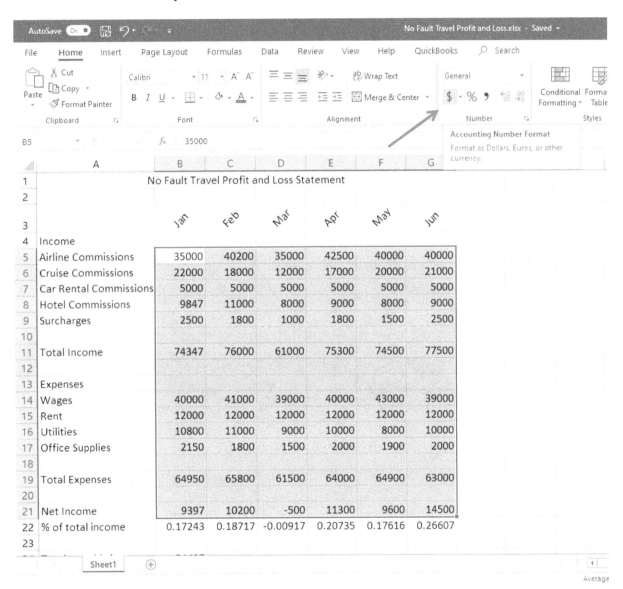

The default accounting style adds both dollars and cents. In this case an even dollar amount is all you need to see. You will now change the formatting to display no values to the right of the decimal point.

2. **Leaving the cells selected, locate and click the Decrease Decimal tool in the Number group twice.**

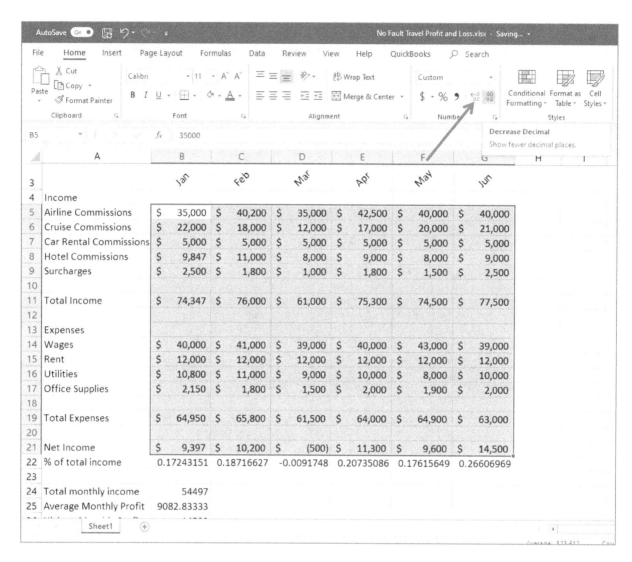

You should now see the numbers displayed in even dollar amounts.

Now you'll add percentage formatting to the percentages you computed using the absolute reference feature.

3. **Select cells B22 through G22.**

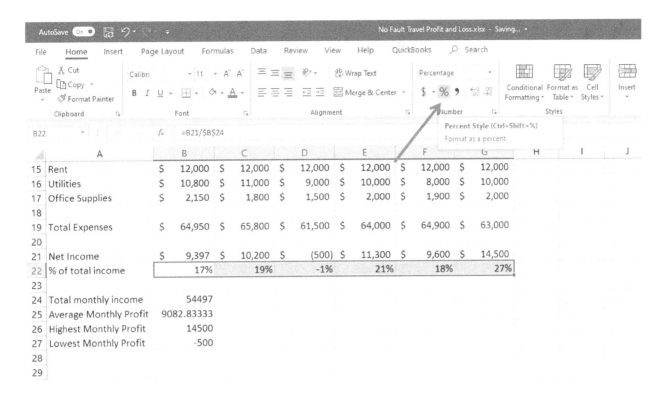

4. Click the Percent style tool in the Number group on the Home tab of the ribbon.

You have now added percentage formatting to these cells. You'll now add two decimal places to increase the accuracy of the percentages.

5. Leaving these cells selected, locate and click the Increase Decimal tool in the numbering group of the Home tab on the ribbon twice.

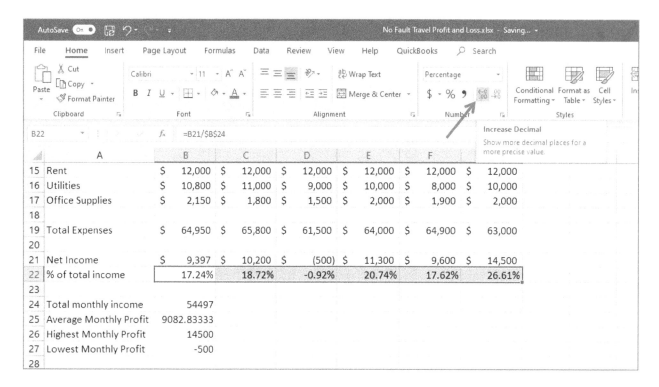

The percentages now display more accurately with two decimal places.

6.   Add Accounting ($) formatting to cells B24 and B27.

This time you'll leave the display at two decimal places for accuracy to the penny.

7.   Save and close the workbook.

Skill Builder: Lesson #4

1.   Open the *Checkbook* workbook.

2.   Center align the labels in row 5.

3.   Insert a new column A, add *Date* as the column heading and enter the dates shown in the illustration.

4.   Apply Accounting style formatting to all cells with dollar amounts.

5.   Delete the empty column G. Adjust the column widths as needed.

6.   When done, your checkbook worksheet should appear similar to the illustration.

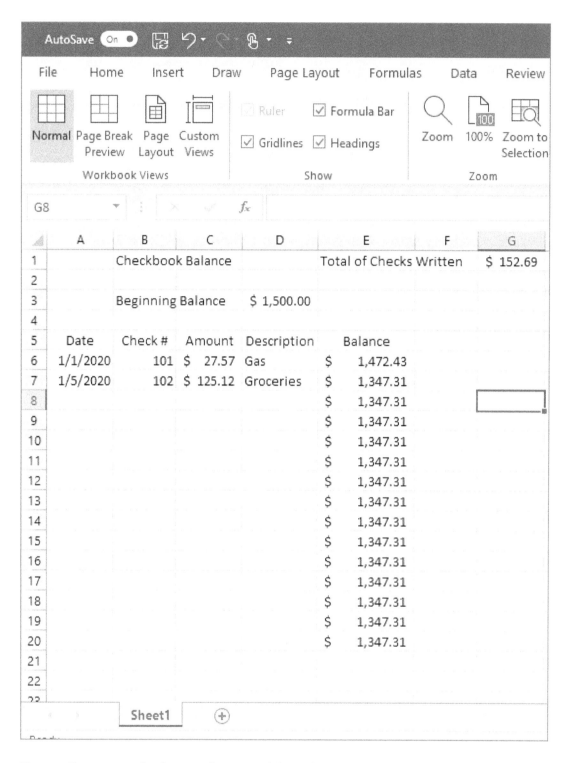

7. **Save and close the workbook.**

Lesson #5: Enhancing Worksheets

In this lesson you will learn to:

> *Change font attributes*
> *Add cell borders*
> *Shade cells*

Lesson #5: Enhancing Worksheets

It is very easy to enhance cells in an Excel worksheet. To enhance cells, first select the cells you wish to enhance. Then, select the enhancement you need either from the ribbon or from the Format dialog box.

1.   Open the *No Fault Travel P&L* workbook.

You'll now add boldfacing to the month names in this worksheet.

2.   Select cells B3 through G3 and then click the Bold tool on the Home tab of the ribbon.

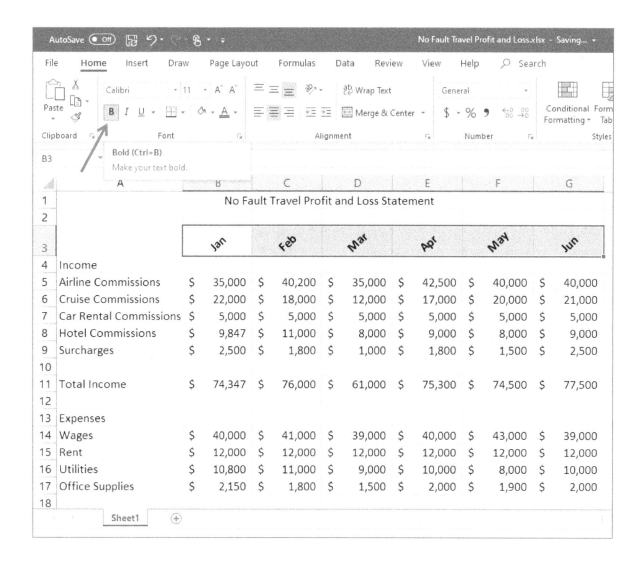

The labels in these cells should be boldfaced.

Now, you'll use a built in Excel style to format the title in cell A1.

3. **Move to cell A1 and click the Cell Styles drop down list. You can find this tool in the Styles group on the Home tab.**

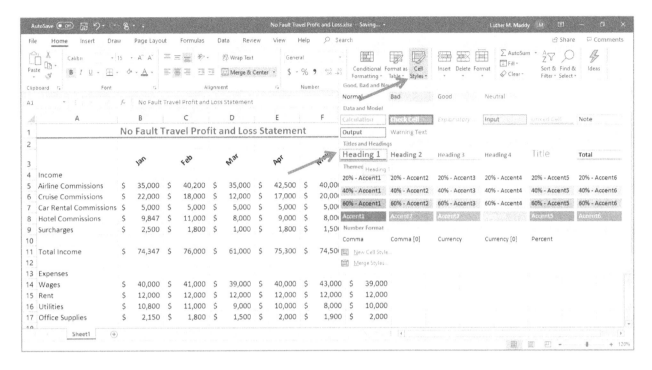

4. **Choose Heading 1 from the styles list.**

Cell A1 should now be formatted in the Heading 1 style. You may not see this style until you move away from cell A1.

You'll now apply a shading cell style to the statistical calculations at the bottom of the worksheet.

5. **Select cells A24 through B27 and then click the Cell Styles drop down list.**

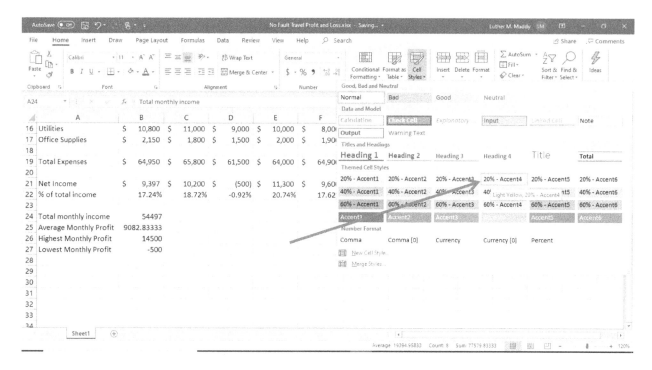

6.   From the list of cell styles, choose 20%-Accent4.

These cells will now be shaded in light orange.

7.   Apply Accounting style formatting to cells B24 through B27.

Adding Cell Borders

To further set off or enhance cells you can easily add borders to cells. You can add top, bottom, left, right, or all four borders. In this portion of the exercise you'll use the Border tool to add a border to the row of cells just above the net profit values.

1.   Select cells A20 through G20.

This is the empty row of cells just above the net profit.

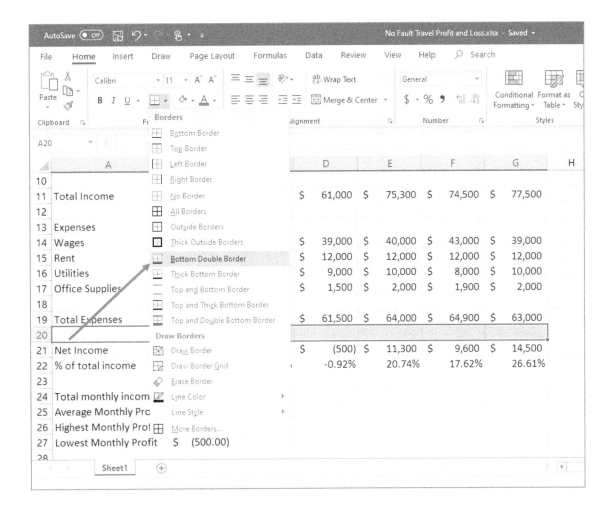

2. Click the Borders drop down list and choose Bottom Double Border.

You will not see the border until you click outside the selected cells. When you do, you should see that Excel has added a double border to those cells.

Using the Format Cells Dialog Box

Excel allows you to change the font face and size. You can also change the color of the text within cells. You can do this from the ribbon. However, using the Format Cells dialog box allows you to preview the font change before actually applying it. You'll now use the Format Cells dialog box to make several changes to some of the cells in this worksheet.

1. Select cells A21 through G21 then click the Format cells dialog box launcher in the Font group of the Home tab.

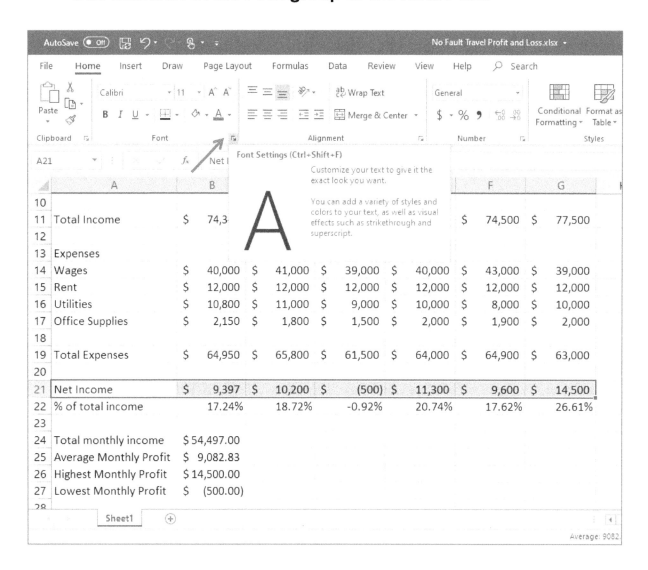

Excel will now display the Format Cells dialog box. Here you can choose from many more formatting options than are available directly on the ribbon.

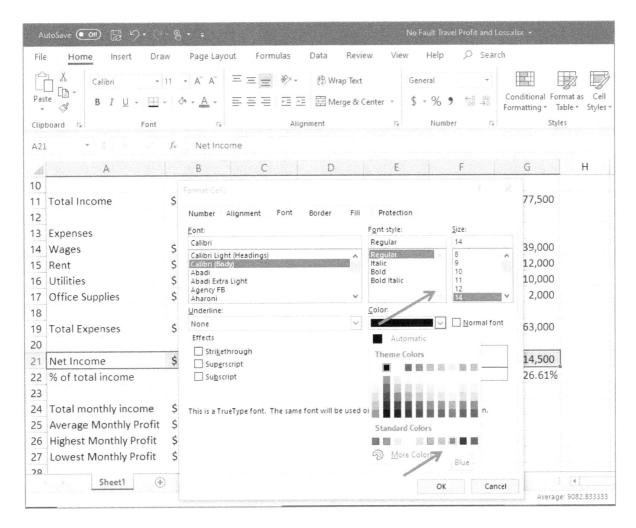

2. Change the font size to 14 points. Then, click the Color drop down list and choose Blue.

After choosing the color, notice that the preview lets you see how the text will appear.

3. Click OK after making these changes.

The net income text should now appear with the enhancements you specified. You will see these changes when you move away from the selected cells.

4. Select cells A19 through G19, the total expenses row.

You will now shade and add line options around to these cells.

5. Launch the Format Cells dialog box.

While the exercise step had you use the Font group, you can launch this dialog box from the Font, Alignment, or Number groups.

Shading Cells

Excel also allows you to add shading to cells or a group of selected cells. When you do add shading to your own worksheets, just be sure to choose a color that will not be so dark that you cannot see the information in a shaded cell.

6. Click the Fill tab in the Format Cells dialog box.

7. Choose light blue for the fill color and then click the Border tab.

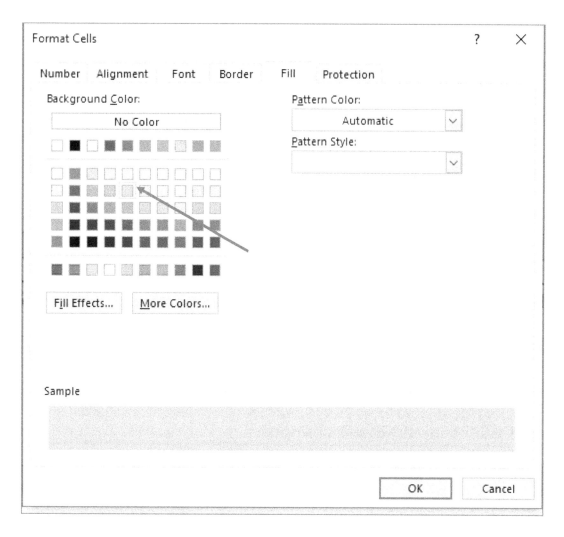

Leave this dialog box open for now.

Cell Borders

You can also add lines or borders to selected cells from this dialog box. When you enter the Borders tab in the Format Cells dialog box you can choose a line style and also choose where and how you want that line style applied.

1. **In the Border tab, choose the sixth Line Style down in the second column.**

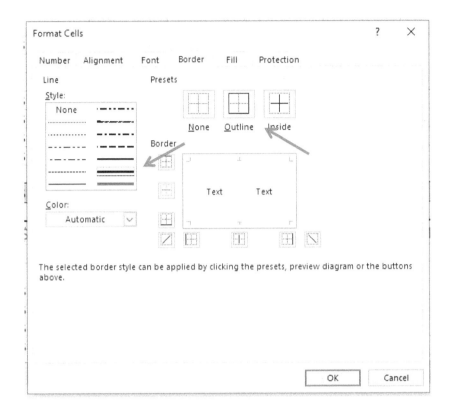

2. **After choosing the Line Style, click the Outline button and click OK.**

You have now informed Excel to place a line around the cells you have selected. If you click anywhere outside the selected cells you will see this change.

The Format Painter

The Format Painter allows you to copy formatting options from one cell to another cell or group of cells. For instance, you just added borders and shading to the cells in row 19. If you want other cells to look the same way, you can use the Format Painter to copy that formatting.

1. **Select cells A19 to G19 again.**

The first step in using the Format Painter is to move into a cell that has the formatting options you want to copy. This could be a single cell, but since this group of cells has a border around the entire group, you need to select all the cells to duplicate the outside border around all the cells you are about to select.

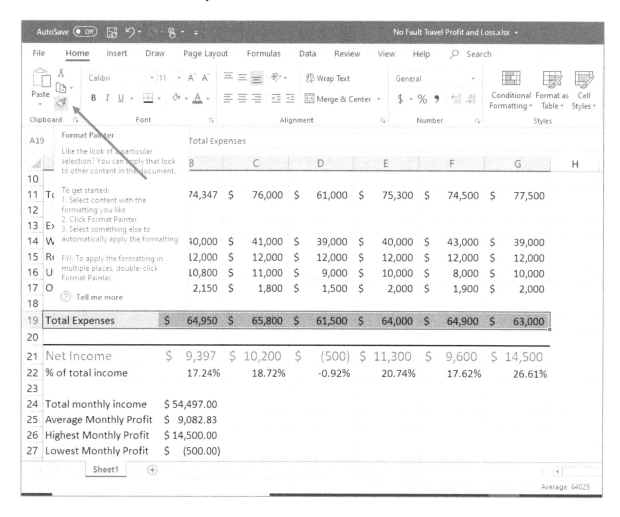

2.   Click the Format Painter tool in the Home tab.

After clicking the Format Painter tool, Excel will apply the formatting to the next cells you select.

3.   Select cells A11 through G11.

You should notice Excel added a paint brush symbol to the mouse pointer.

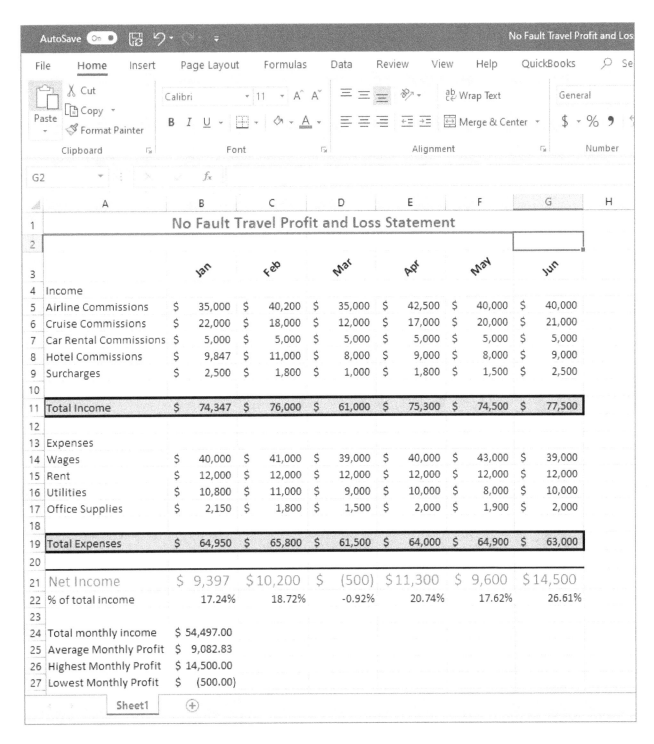

Your worksheet should now appear similar to the above after adding the cell styles and other enhancements.

4.   Save and close this workbook when done.

Skill Builder: Lesson #5

1. **Open the *Checkbook* workbook.**

2. **Make the changes needed so that your worksheet appears as the one below, including the amount of the first check. Choose the shading style/color of your choice.**

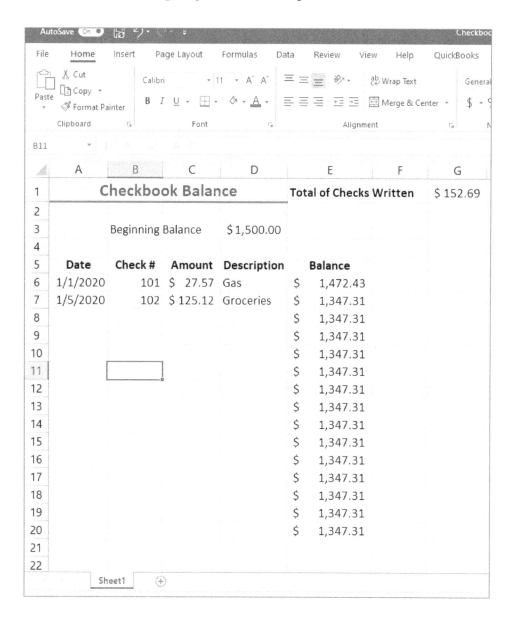

3. **Save, then close the *Checkbook* worksheet.**

Lesson #6: Printing Features

In this lesson you will learn to:
Use Print Preview
Add Headers & Footers
Print Gridlines

Lesson #6: Printing Features

Printing is a very easy feature. Because worksheets may be quite large, most of the time you may not want to print the entire worksheet. In this lesson you will learn how to specify only certain parts of the worksheet for printing. You will also learn to add features such as headers and footers.

1. Open the *No Fault Travel* workbook.

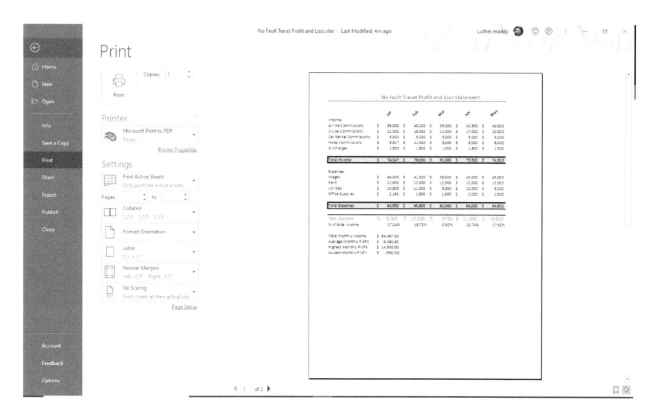

2. Open the File menu and choose Print.

Printing a Worksheet

Choosing the Print command box allows you to select certain portions of the worksheet and even which pages to print. You can also see a preview of the printed worksheet. Clicking the Print tool on the toolbar automatically prints the entire worksheet. The other options in this menu include letting you specify what portions of the worksheet you would like to print, how many copies to print, and what printer to use when printing.

Notice that the print preview shows the data that will not fit on the first page. As it is now, this worksheet takes two pages to print. You can verify this by examining the page indicator near the bottom center of the screen.

3.   **Click the Next Page arrow** _____ **at the bottom of the print preview area.**

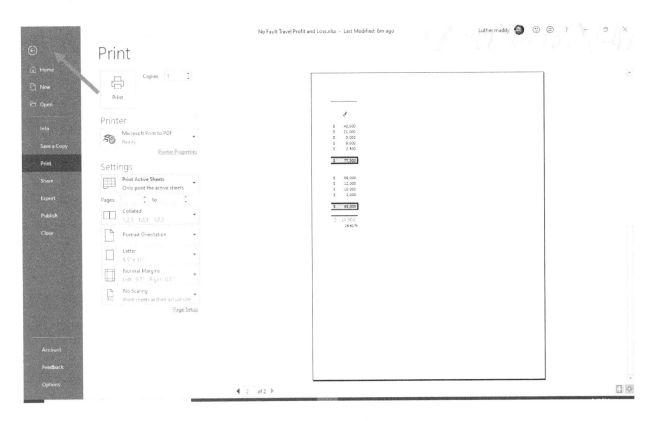

You now see the information that would print on the second page.

4.   **After viewing the Print Preview, click the Back arrow at the top left of the File menu to return to the worksheet.**

Adjusting Print Options

If you want this entire spreadsheet to fit on one page you can shrink the font and column widths on the worksheet. Or, you could tell Excel to shrink the information to have it fit on one page. You could also change the page orientation to Landscape. We'll first have you tell Excel to fit this all on one portrait page.

Returning to the worksheet you should notice that Excel has added a dotted vertical line on your worksheet between columns F and G. This line represents a page break. From your screen, or the image below, you should clearly see that column G will not print on the first page of the worksheet.

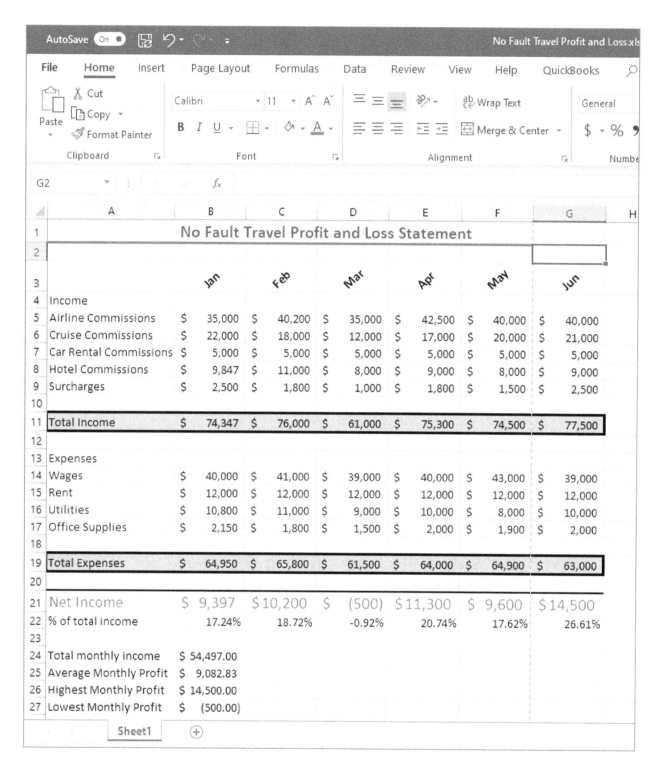

You will now inform Excel that you want to fit the worksheet on just one page.

1.   Click the dialog box launcher on the Page Setup group on the Page Layout tab.

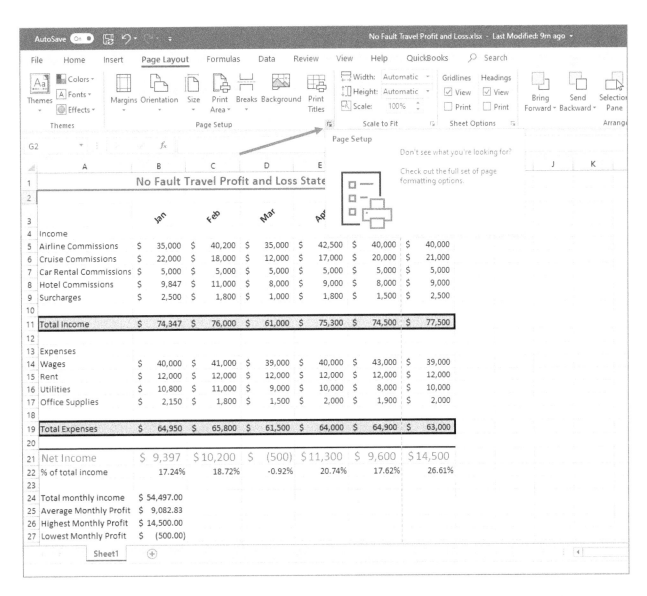

You can click the launcher from either the Page Setup, Scale to Fit, or Sheet Options group in the Page Setup on the ribbon.

You should now see the Page Setup dialog box. Many of the options available here are also available on the Ribbon.

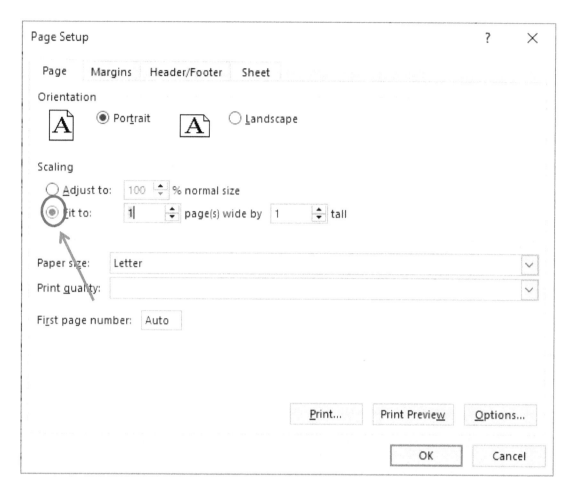

2. **If needed, click the Page tab in the Page Setup dialog box. Next, click the Fit to radio button and ensure the options are 1 page wide by 1 page tall.**

You have now given Excel the command to shrink all the data in this worksheet to fit on one page during the printing process.

3. **Click OK to leave this dialog box.**

You should notice the page break between column F and G is gone. You could have also changed this setting by using the ribbon. In the Scale to Fit group you should now see that the width is set as 1 page, as is the height. You can change this setting by using the drop-down arrow for each of these tools.

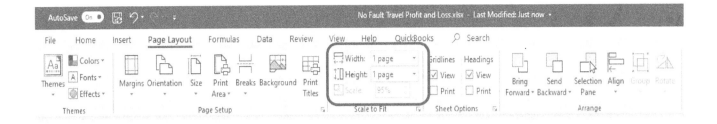

4. Click File to open the File menu and choose Print.

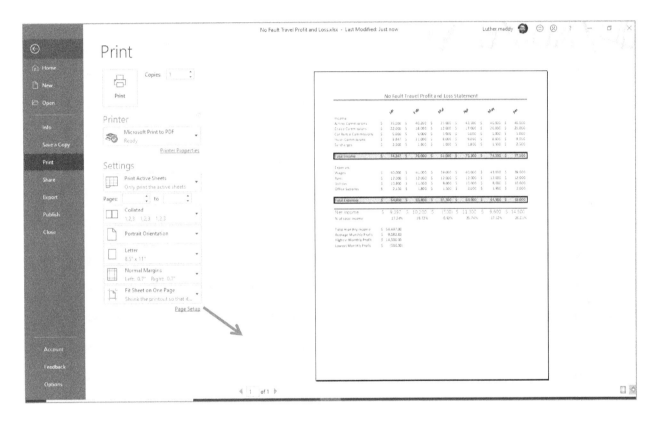

You should see that the entire worksheet is displayed and will fit on one page.

Printing a Partial Worksheet

As you have just seen, Excel prints the entire worksheet unless you tell it otherwise. If you do not wish to print the entire worksheet, first select the cells you want to print. Then, open the File menu, but before selecting print you will choose Print Selection in the settings section. In this portion of the lesson, you will specify that only a portion of the worksheet prints.

1.   Return to the worksheet and then select cells A1 through G11.

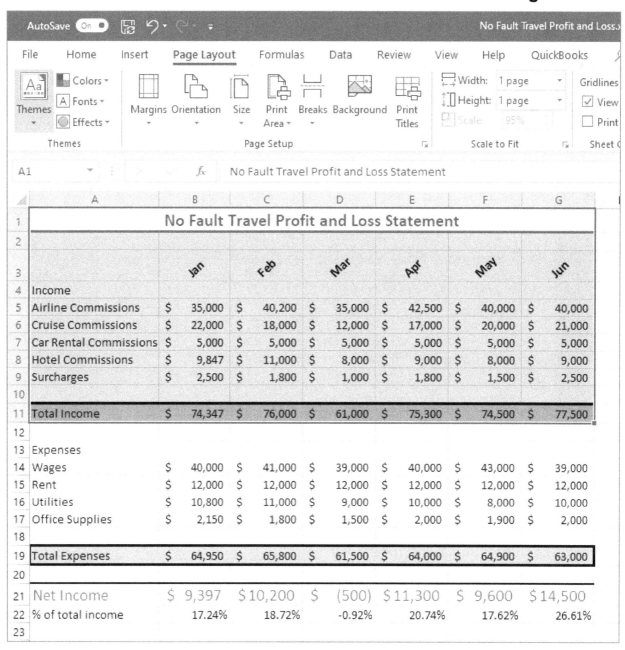

2.   Click File, then choose Print.

Notice that according to the Print Preview section, the entire worksheet will be printed. You need to inform Excel that you only want to print the cells you have selected.

3.   In the Settings section, choose Print Selection.

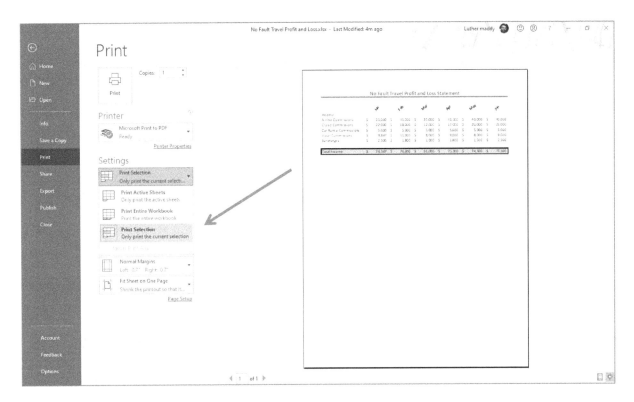

After selecting this option, as you examine the preview, you should notice that only the selected cells are displayed. If you had chosen to print to a printer, the result on paper would be the same.

5.   Return to the worksheet by clicking the left arrow at the top left instead of actually printing.

For this lesson, you will save paper and ink as you explore Excel's printing features by not actually printing the worksheet.

Changing the Orientation

By default, Excel chooses to print this worksheet information in portrait orientation. Turning the page sideways (landscape) allows you to print more columns. In this portion of the lesson you will change the orientation to landscape and observe the changes.

1.   **In the Scale to Fit group, change the width and height back to Automatic by clicking the drop-down arrow in each section.**

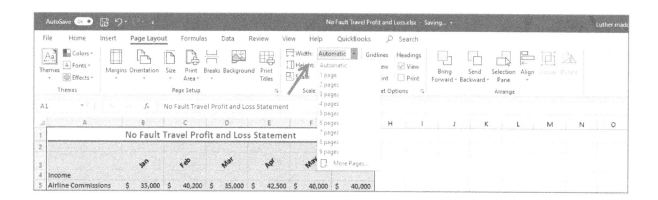

As you changed the width and height options, you should notice that Excel now displays where the page break again between columns F and G.

You will now change the orientation to landscape. This will allow more columns to fit across the page when the worksheet is printed.

2.   **In the Page Setup tab, click the Orientation tool and choose Landscape.**

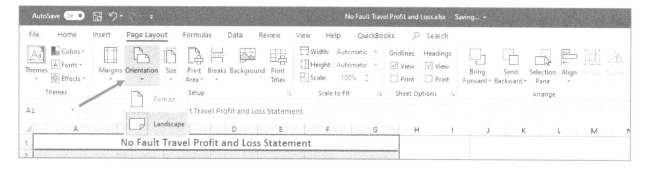

When you returned to the worksheet, notice that Excel has moved the page break over a couple of rows. This reflects the change in orientation to landscape.

You can also change the orientation and several other options by going into the Page Setup dialog box or even when after you have selected the Print command. There is no one "right way" to select Excel commands.

4.   **Click File and choose Print.**

Notice the preview section shows the orientation change.

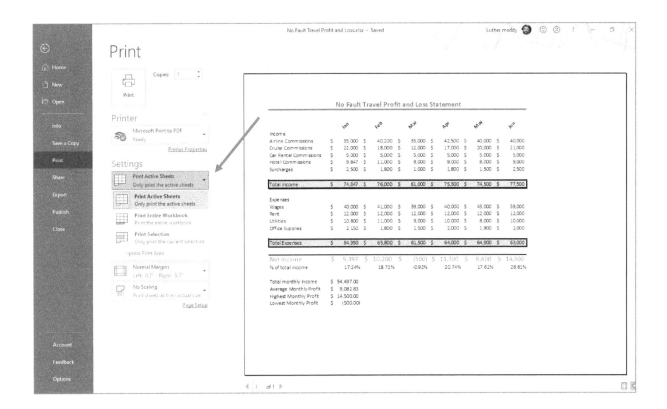

5. Change the Print Settings back to Print Active Sheet from Print Selection.

As you view print options you should notice that Landscape orientation is selected. You could have also changed the orientation here without having to return to the worksheet.

Adding Headers and Footers

As you examined the print preview you may have noticed the absence of page numbers. By default, Excel does not add page numbers and other information at the top or bottom of the page. In this portion of the lesson you will add header and footer information, including page numbers to the printout.

1. Close the Print menu and return to the worksheet. Then, click the Page Setup dialog box launcher again.

There are many pre-defined headers and footers which in most cases will give you the exact options you need. However, we'll have you create headers and footers from scratch so you can learn more about their use.

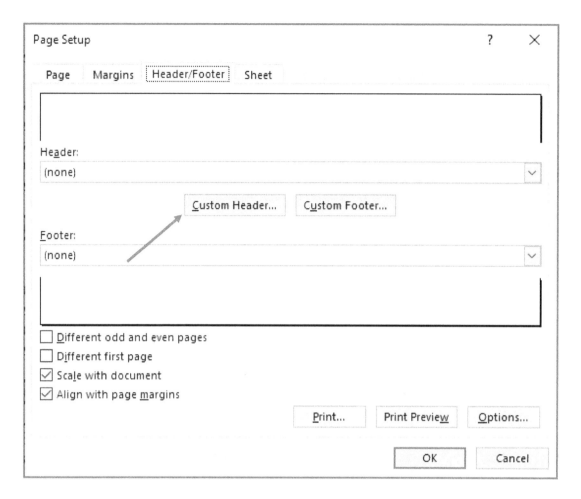

2. In the Page Setup dialog box, click the Header/Footer tab then click the Custom Header button.

You should now see the Header dialog box which consists of three sections: left, right, and center. There are tools in this dialog box to insert Excel generated items in the header like the page number, file name, and current date. You can also type custom text in any of the three sections.

3. Press (Tab) twice to move to the Right section of the header.

4. **In the Right section of the header type *Printed on:* and then insert a (Space).**

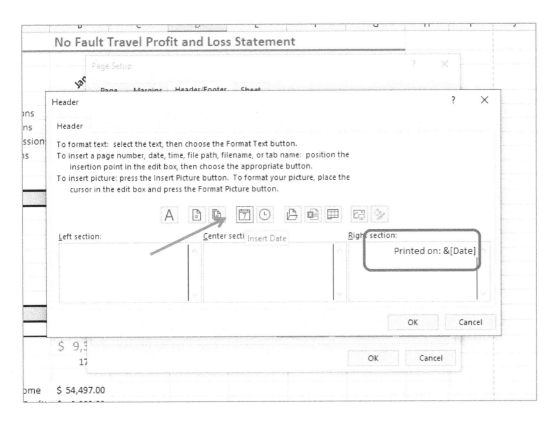

5. **Click the Insert Date tool in the Header dialog box.**

You should now see &[Date] in the right section. When you print, Excel will add the current date. You should use the Date code rather than typing the date so that the date on the printout will let you know exactly how current the spreadsheet printout is.

In addition to creating a custom header or footer as you just did, Excel has several pre-created headers and footers you may be able to use. In this portion of the exercise you will use a pre-created footer.

6. **Click OK to return to the Header/Footer tab.**

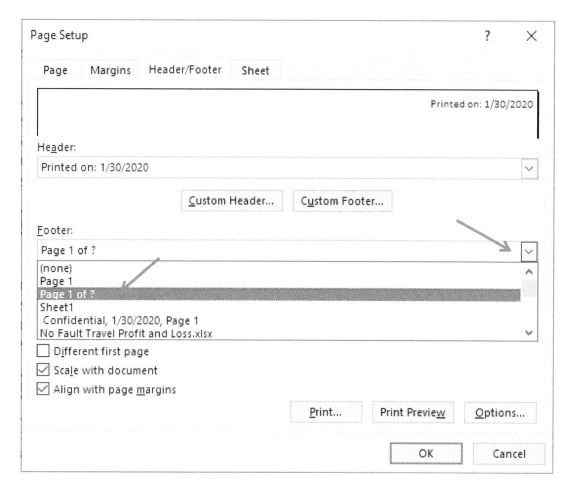

7.   Click the Footer drop-down list button, choose *Page 1 of ?* and then click OK.

The header and footers you just added to your worksheet will not display on the worksheet. They will appear when you print the worksheet or view it in Print Preview.

8.   Click File and then choose Print.

9. In the Print menu, change the Settings to print Active sheets instead of Selection.

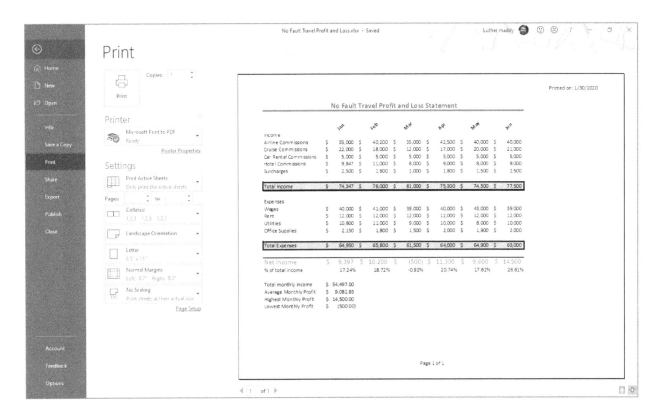

You should see the header and footer in the print preview.

The Page Layout View

If you want to see options normally not visible in the editing mode, like headers and footers, you can change the view to the Page Layout view. In this mode you can work with your worksheet as well as see headers, footers, and a better representation of page breaks.

1. Return to the worksheet from the Print menu and then click the View tab.

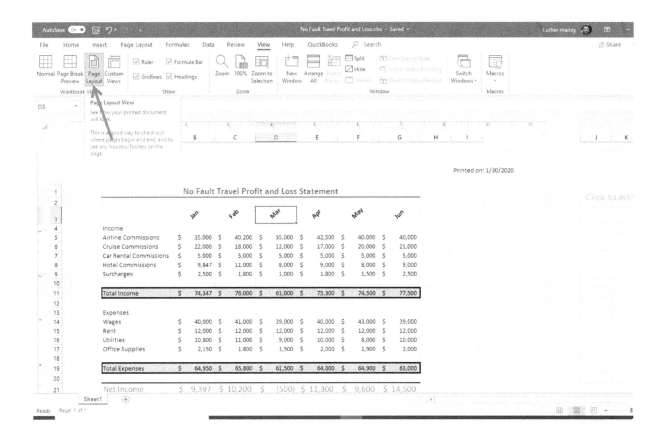

2. In the View tab, click the Page Layout tool in the Workbook Views group.

You should now see the header and footer you just created.

The Page Layout view allows you to work with the worksheet as does the Normal view. The difference is that you can see page formatting options.

3. In the View tab, click the Normal tool in the Workbook Views group.

Excel has now returned to the Normal view.

Printing Gridlines

As you examined the print preview, you may have noticed that the only lines that appear are the ones you added to the worksheet. It is possible to have Excel print gridlines around each cell. With gridlines added, the printout will resemble the layout of the actual worksheet as you work with it. You can add gridlines from Page Setup.

1. Click the Page Layout tab and launch the Page Setup dialog box.

2. In the Page Setup dialog box, click the Sheet tab.

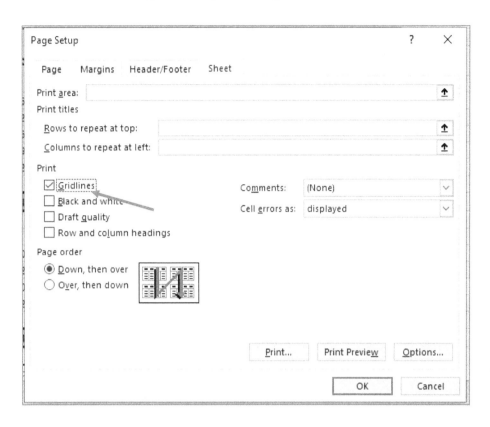

3. In the Sheet tab, click the Gridlines check box and click OK.

4. Click the File tab again and choose Print.

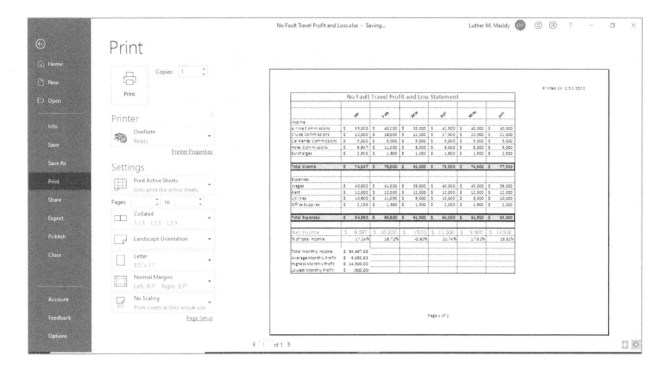

You should now see that Excel added cell gridlines to the print preview.

4.   Save and close the *No Fault Travel P&L* workbook.

Skill Builder: Lesson #6

1.   Open the Checkbook worksheet.

2.   Use Print Preview and Page Setup to add the current date and Page 1 of ? to the header as shown below:

To do this easily you can start with the pre-defined header that displays Page 1 of X, then select Custom Header and add the Date code.

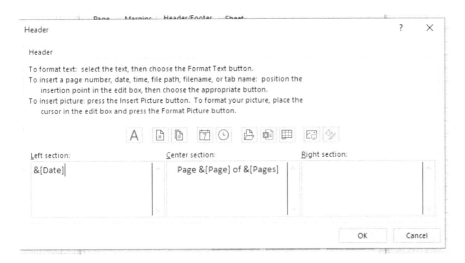

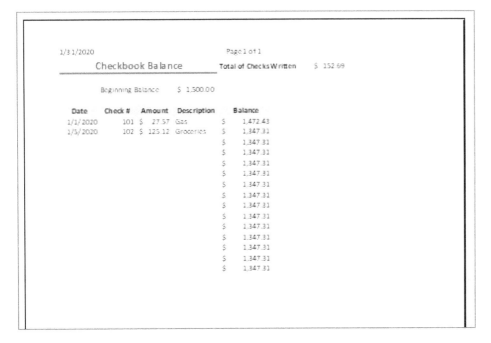

3.   Save and close the *Checkbook* worksheet.

Lesson #7: Creating Graphs

In this lesson you will learn to:

> *Create Graphs and Charts*
> *Modify Charts*
> *Add a Trendline*

Lesson #7: Creating Graphs

After you have created a spreadsheet and entered data in it, you can easily use Excel to create charts and graphs of that information. In this lesson you will use Excel's chart feature to create graphs.

The first step in creating a chart is to decide what you want to graph and what kind of chart you want to use. Not all data is compatible with all chart types, for example, Pie Charts are useful in displaying the makeup of an entire unit. Column and Bar charts are useful for comparisons and Line charts are most often used for viewing a trend over time. There are also variations within each major chart category.

After deciding what kind of chart to use, you should then make sure you have the correct values in the workbook. After ensuring this, the next step is to select the cells that you want the graph to chart. After doing this, you will then choose the chart category you wish to insert from the Charts group on the Insert tab.

1.   Open the No Fault Travel P&L workbook.

You will now create a column chart that displays each month's net income.

2.   Select cells A3 through G3.

You selected the month names that will appear as the column labels on this chart. You started with column A because you want a label from column A in the range of values you are about to select to also appear on the chart.

3.   Press and hold the (Control) key and then click and drag to select cells A21 through G21.

Holding down the (control) key allows you to select two separate (non-contiguous) cell ranges in this worksheet. You included the label, "Net Income" in column A as well as the month's net incomes because this label should appear on the graph.

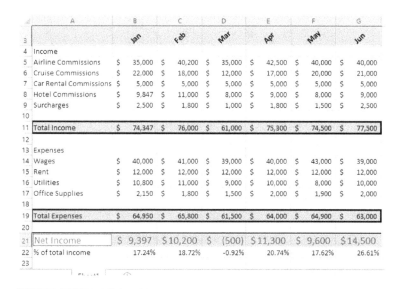

4.   With these cells selected, click the Insert tab, then click Column in the Charts group.

Now you can choose the type of chart you want and other options very easily.

5.   In the Column style, choose the first sub chart in the 2D column group, Clustered Column.

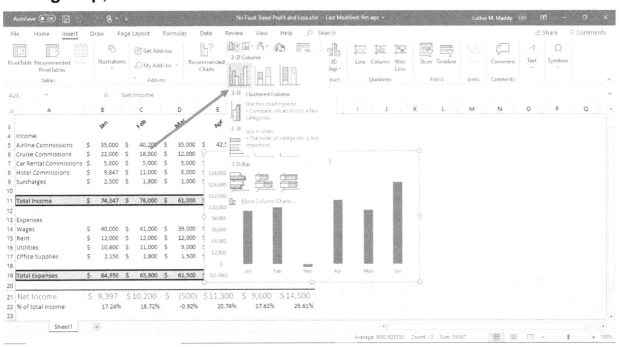

As you can see here, there are several varieties of charts you can create. Excel will build your chart for you on the active worksheet as a floating object. As a floating object, you can move the chart to a new location and change its size. In this lesson however, you will move the chart to a sheet by itself. This allows you to see that chart as it will appear when printed alone. If you want to print the data and the chart, then leaving it on the worksheet with the values you are graphing is a good idea.

Moving a chart

We will now move the chart to a separate worksheet so it no longer interferes with the worksheet data.

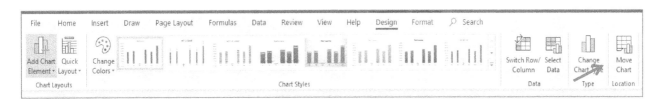

6. **Click the Design tab from Chart Tools, then click the Move Chart tool. Select the "New sheet" option and then click OK.**

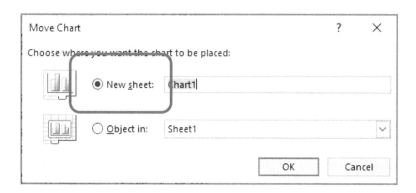

The Move Chart dialog box also allows you to name the chart sheet. Naming and working with multiple worksheets is covered in the next level workbook. By default, Excel will name the first chart, Chart1 and increment the name as you add additional charts.

You should now see the completed chart in a sheet by itself. If you examine the sheet tabs at the bottom of the window, you will see that Excel added a tab labeled Chart1. The Sheet1 worksheet contains the data you used to create the chart. Clicking a tab's name switches to that sheet.

Data Labels

Among the many enhancements you can add to Excel charts are data labels. Data Labels allow you to add the value or information for each column of the chart. You will now add Data labels to the top of each column in this chart.

7.   Ensure the Design tab is active then click the Add Chart Element tool, select Data Labels and then choose Outside End.

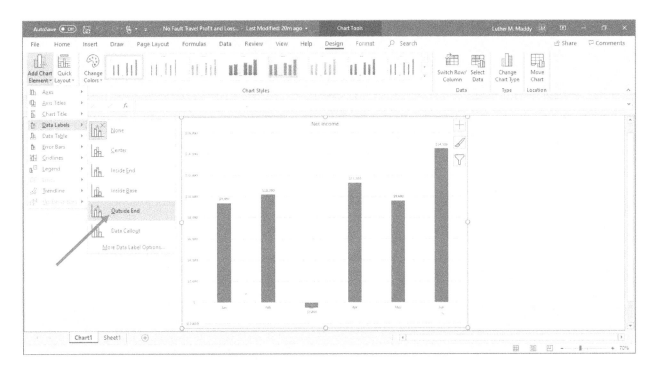

You should see that Excel added a value just outside the end of each column.

Modifying a Chart

After you have created a chart, you may wish to change its appearance. For example, you may want to use different colors or change fonts or make other changes.

Altering elements on an existing graph is very easy. In this portion of the lesson, you will change the appearance of this graph.

1.   Click on any of the monthly columns in this chart.

You should notice that all of the bars now have small circles at their tops and bottoms. This lets you know that you have selected all the bars, not just one single bar.

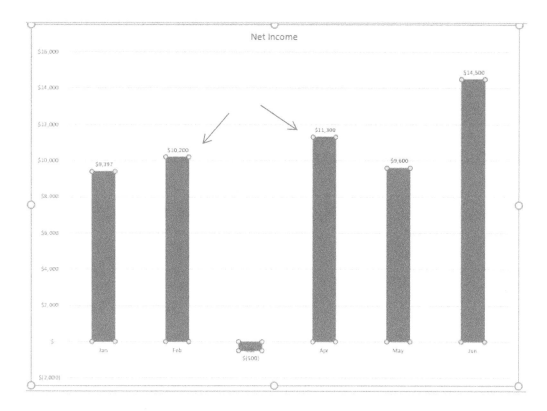

The sizing handles (the small circles at the top and bottom of the columns) tell you this element of the chart is selected. Any formatting changes you make will affect the selected element, in this case the columns.

2. Click the Change Colors tool on the Design tab.

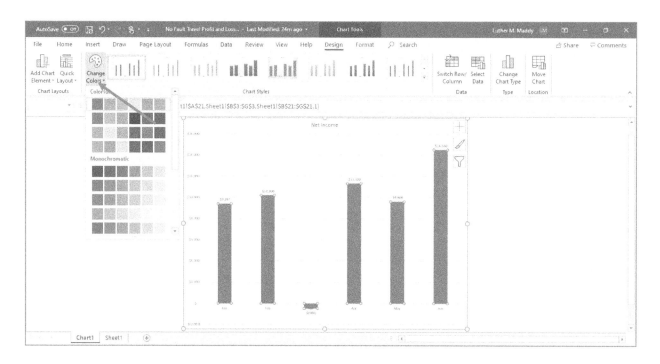

You will now see colors available to fill the columns with. In addition to choosing a color here, you can also experiment with additional Fill options such as adding a texture or gradient fill style. For now, you'll just change the color of the chart columns.

3. In the colors available, click Green, Colorful Palette 4 in the first column of color schemes, fourth row down.

The columns in the color schemes represent series at each data point. There is only one data series here, net income, so the first color in the color scheme row changes all the columns in the chart to that color. You will work with multiple data series shortly.

Every column in the chart should now have changed to the green color. Next, you'll enhance the appearance of the data labels by first selecting them and then applying the enhancement.

4. Click on one of the values (data labels) above any column.

You should see sizing handles around all the data labels, informing you that this element is now selected. You will now change the font size of the data labels.

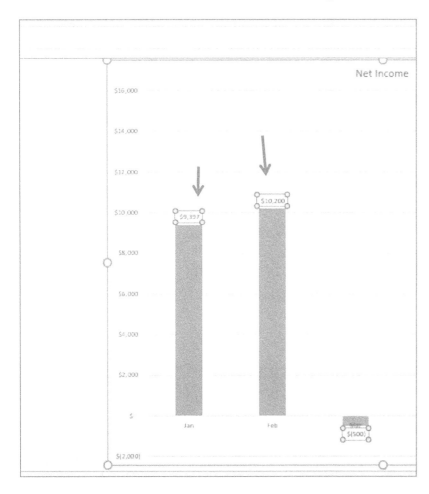

5. **Display the Home tab and then click the Font Size drop down list. Choose 14 points as the font size.**

The data labels should now be larger, displaying in 14 point type.

Now, you'll change the size of this chart's title.

6. **Click the chart's title to select it.**

Once again the sizing handles tell you the title is selected.

7. **Use the Font Size drop down list and change the font size to 20 points.**

The title should now display in 20-point type.

The graph is now complete. When you save the worksheet, Excel will also save the graph. The graph is also dynamic. This means that it will change automatically if the data on the worksheet changes. You will now change data on the worksheet and verify that the graph does change.

8. **Click the Sheet1 tab to return to the *No Fault Travel P&L* worksheet.**

9. **Change cell D6, March Cruise Commissions, to *$15,000*.**

10. **Click on the Chart1 sheet tab and view the graph.**

The graph has instantly changed to reflect the new values in the worksheet.

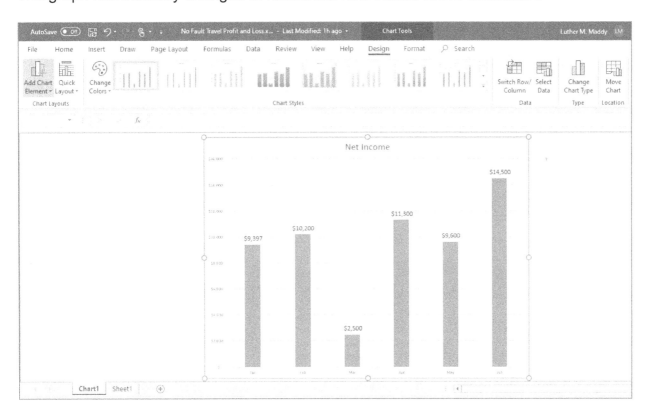

Working with Chart Types

Even after creating a chart, you can still change the type if you want. To do this, select the chart object, then display the Design tab and choose Change Chart type. Excel will then display the types of charts available. In this portion of the exercise you will change the chart type to Line.

1.   Display the Design tab and click the Change Chart Type tool.

You should now see the Change Chart Type dialog box.

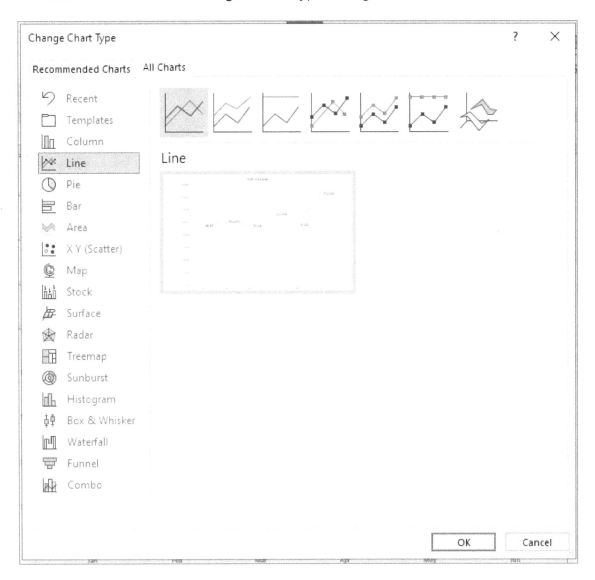

2.   In the Change Chart Type dialog box, choose Line as the chart type. Choose the first subtype and click OK.

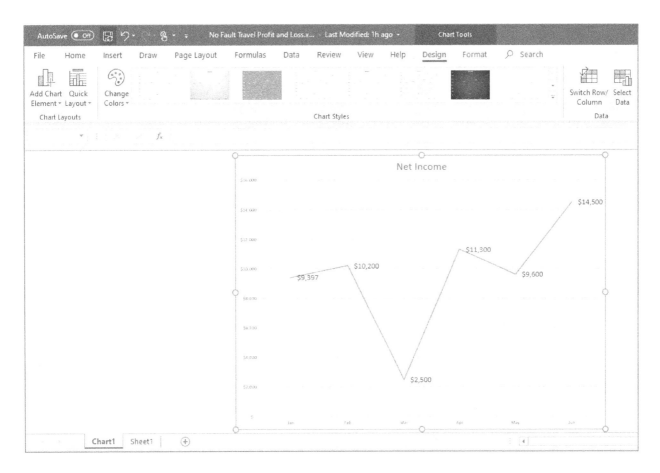

Excel has now changed the chart into a line chart. Line charts are most often used to graphically display trends.

You will now change the chart back to a column chart so you can add a trend line, another very useful feature of creating charts in Excel. Trendlines cannot be added to line charts, so you'll change the chart type back to column.

3. Click the Change Chart Type tool again and change the chart type back to Column.

Choose the first sub type (not 3-D) in the first column.

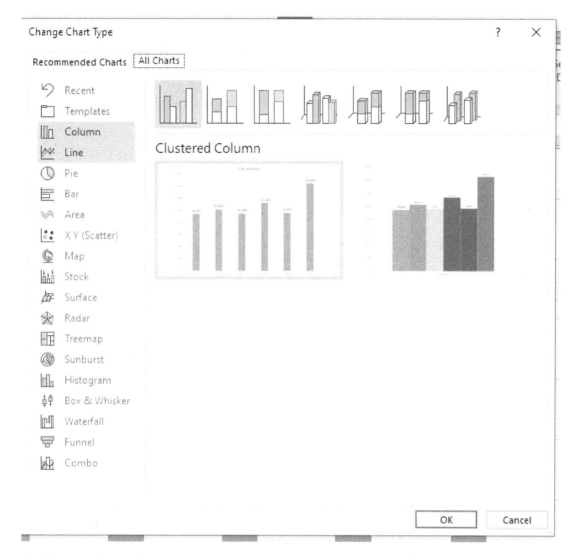

Adding a Trendline

If you are using a 2-D chart, you can have Excel compute and graph a trendline. Excel will not add trendlines to 3-D charts. To add a trendline you must first select the data series for which you want to compute a trendline. In this chart there is only one data series. After selecting the data series, choose Trend Line in the Chart Tools group.

1.   **While viewing the chart, click the Add Chart Element tool and then select Trendline.**

2.   From the list of trendlines, choose the Linear option.

You should now see that Excel has computed and charted a trendline for the net profit. Depending on your monitor and color scheme, the trendline may appear very lightly in the chart.

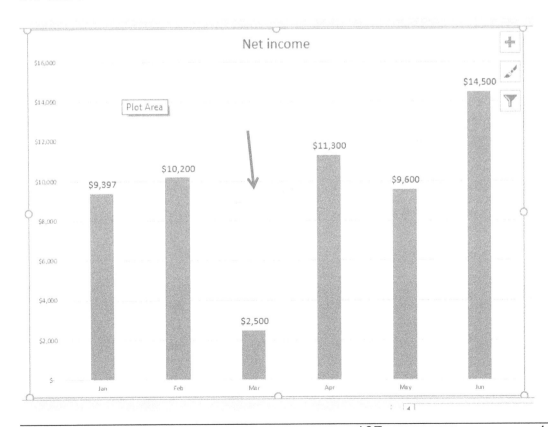

Charting Multiple Data Series

The chart you just created has only one set of columns or data series. If you need to chart more than one data series, simply select all the data then choose a chart type. In this portion of the lesson you will create a chart that graphs all of the income categories. Since there is more than one income category, the result will be multiple data series on this chart.

1.   Click on the Sheet1 tab to return to the No Fault Travel worksheet.

2.   Select A3 through G9.

Do not select row 11.

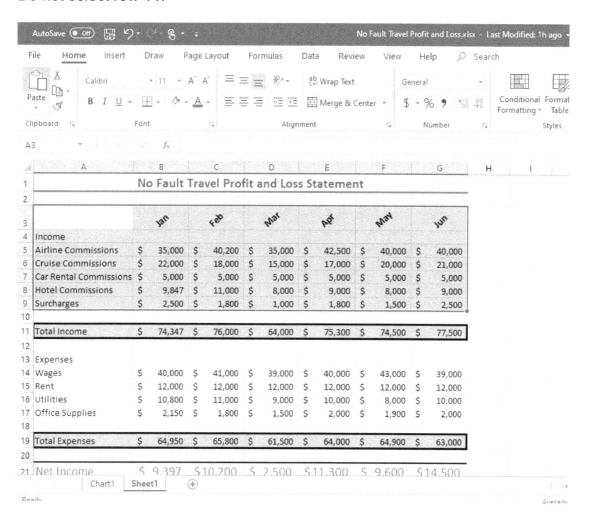

You have included the labels in column A and row 3 so they will also be included on the chart.

3. Display the Insert tab then click Column in the Chart group. Select the first 2D column chart

You have selected a 2D column chart, the same type you used for the other chart.

Excel automatically adds the column chart to the worksheet with the values. You will move it to a sheet by itself like the other chart.

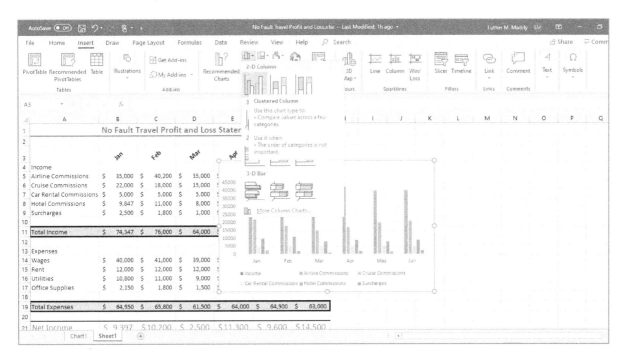

4. Click the Move Chart tool on the Design tab and choose to move the chart to a new sheet.

Notice that the sheet for this chart will be automatically named Chart2.

You should now see the column chart with multiple data series. You will now change the chart type to a stacked column chart.

5.   Ensure the Design tab is displayed, then click the Change Chart Type tool.

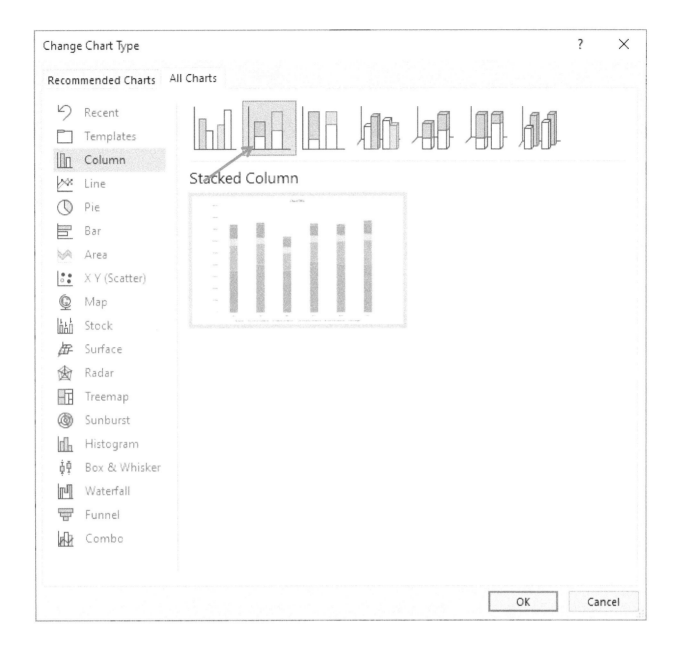

6. **Choose Column as the Chart type. Choose Stacked Column, the second one in the first row as the sub-type, and click OK.**

You should now see that Excel has created a stacked column chart from the data series you selected.

Creating a Pie Chart

Pie charts are most often used to display the makeup of a whole. In this portion of the lesson you will create a pie chart that graphs the total net income (profit) for this six month period and the contribution of each month. The total income for the period will represent the entire pie and each month will be a slice of the pie. After you have created the pie chart, you'll add some additional enhancements to it.

1.   **Return to Sheet1 and select cells A3:G3 and A21:G21.**

Remember that pressing and holding the (Control) key allows you to select these two noncontiguous ranges. As you did with the other charts, you've included labels that will appear on the chart.

2.   **On the Insert tab, click the Pie Chart tool and then choose the first 3-D pie chart.**

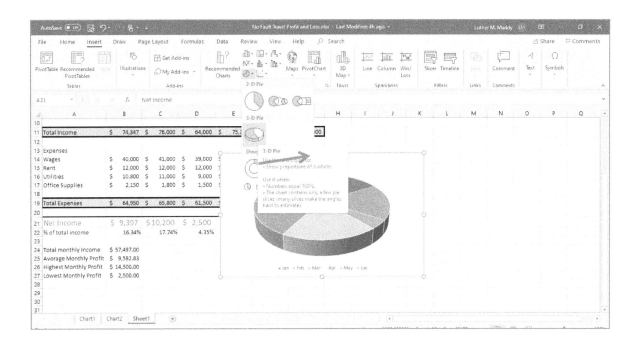

3.   Move the chart to a new worksheet.

In addition to clicking the Move Chart tool on the Design tab, you could also right+click the chart and choose Move Chart from the shortcut menu. Excel should label this sheet Chart3.

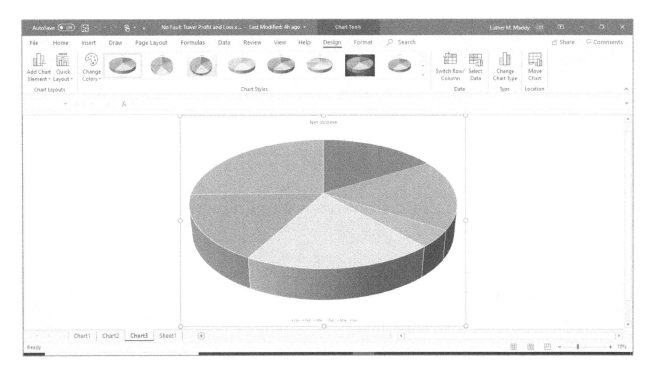

Notice the labels you included in the selected cells appear as the legend and chart title.

Formatting charts

You'll now use some of Excel's formatting features to change the appearance of this 3-D pie chart. In this process you'll add data labels, remove the legend, and change the 3-D appearance.

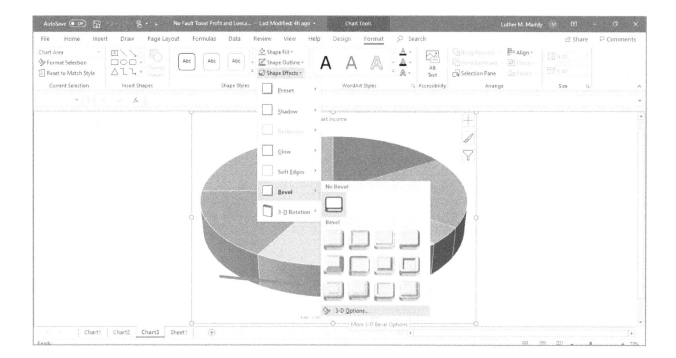

4. **Click the pie chart to select it. Then, display the Format tab then click the Shape Effects tool.**

You will know the chart is selected because you will see sizing handles around the pie chart. You are looking for sizing handles around the slices of the pie chart, not just the entire chart.

5. **From the Shape Effects options submenu, choose Bevel and then 3-D Options.**

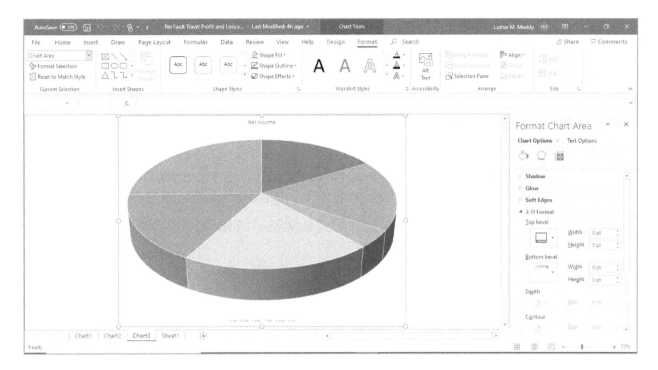

You should now see the Format Data Series pane along the right of the Excel window. If the title is not Format Data Series, close it and repeat Steps 4 and 5 above, ensuring the chart is selected.

6. **Change the four width and height settings in the Top Bevel section to 600 points and then close the Format Data Series pane by clicking the "X" to the right of its title.**

These settings control how large or small the bevel will be on the chart. Changing them all to 600 points gives the chart a very interesting appearance.

You'll now remove the legend and add data labels.

7.   Display the Design tab, click the Add Chart Element tool and then choose Legend. From the available options, choose None.

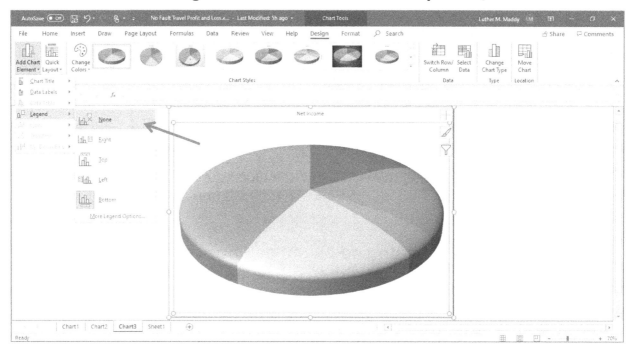

Now that the legend is gone, there is no way to identify the slices of pie. You'll add data labels that display the month name and also the percentage of profit that month contributes to the whole.

However, instead of having to create a formula using absolute reference as you did earlier, Excel's charting feature will automatically compute the percentage for you when you create a pie chart.

8.   Click the Add Chart Element tool and choose Data Labels. Then from the Data Labels submenu, choose More Data Label Options.

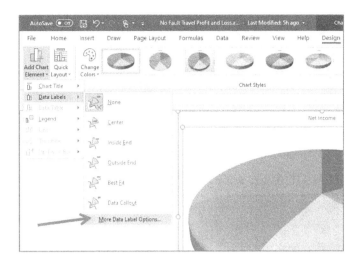

You should now see the Format Data Labels pane on the right of the Excel window. Here you can specify many formatting options for data labels.

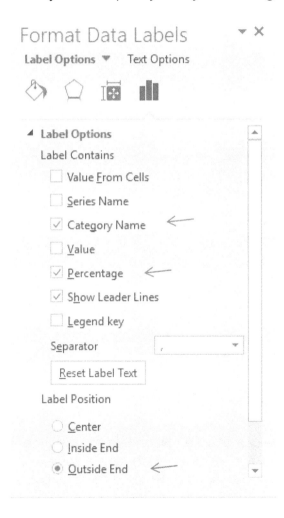

9. **In the Format Data Labels pane, select Category Name, and Percentage check boxes in the Label Contains section. Turn off all other Label Contains options.**

10. **Choose Outside End as the Label Position and click Close the Format Data Labels pane by clicking the X.**

11. **Move to the Home tab and change the size of the data labels to 16 points.**

You can do this by ensuring the data labels are selected and then changing the font size on the home tab.

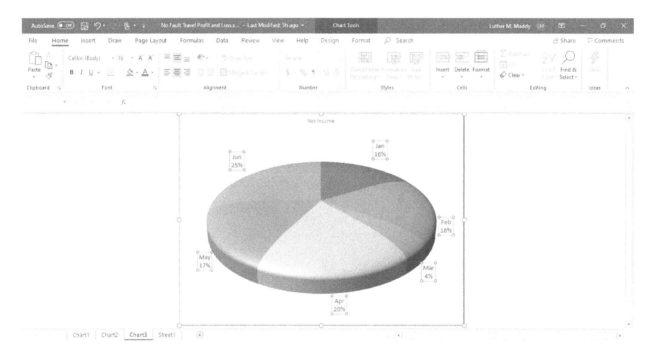

You have now created a pie chart and changed its appearance. This image shows the chart with the formatting pane closed.

11. **Save and close the *No Fault Travel P&L* Workbook.**

Congratulations! You have completed the Excel Basics course. Now, take a little time to practice the concepts you have learned with your own values. Then, when you are ready to learn some additional features, you can start Excel 2016 Beyond the Basics to help you become even more productive with Excel.

Index

Other MS Office workbooks that may interest you
versions for 2010, 2013, 2016, & 2019 available

These workbooks work great in the classroom or for learning on your own.

Access: The Basics

This course will give users a firm grasp of the basics of MS Access. Users will learn to: Understand Basic Database Design Techniques, Create, Modify and Use Tables, Create and Modify Forms, Create and Modify Reports and Mailing Labels, Create Database Relationships, Find and Edit Records, Create and Use Queries, and add Drop-down Lists to Forms

Access: Beyond the Basics

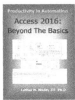

This course will give you a firm grasp of many useful Access features beyond the essentials. In this course will learn to: Use lookup fields and table validation rules, Work with filters, Understand and modify join properties, Add calculations to queries, forms and reports, Create and use Macros, Create and use parameter and action queries, Create and use subforms.

Excel: Beyond the basics

Learn to create advanced formulas using Excel functions like PMT(), IF(), VLookup() and more. You will also learn about worksheet protection, data validation, creating and using templates, advanced charting features, and much more.

Excel 2016: Database and Statistical Features

Learn to create and use Pivot Tables and Charts. You'll also learn about database functions like DSum() and DAverage(). You'll also learn about filtering and subtotaling Excel data. Finally, you'll learn about performing statistical analysis using the Analysis Toolpak.

PowerPoint: The Basics

In this "learning by doing" course you will learn to: Create and run presentations, Apply and modify design themes, Insert clipart, audio, and video clips, Apply and use slide transitions, Print audience handouts and speaker notes and much more

Also: Word: The Basics & Word: Enhancing Documents

Order wherever books are sold.

Ordering in quantity? Save up 20% by ordering directly: Contact the author at: www.LutherMaddy.com